Gotta Minute

MW01244805

to...

Best wishes,

Tom May

The
ABC's
of
Successful
Living

Getting What You Really Want

by Tom Massey, Ph.D., N.D.

Robert D. Reed Publishers • San Francisco, California

Robert D. Reed Publishers
750 La Playa Street, Suite 647
San Francisco, CA 94121
Phone: 650/994-6570 • Fax: 650/994-6579
E-mail: 4bobreed@msn.com
Web site: www.rdrpublishers.com

Designed and typeset by Katherine Hyde
Cover designed by Julia A. Gaskill at Graphics Plus

ISBN 1-885003-76-5

Library of Congress Control Number 00-109040

Produced and Printed in the United States of America

Foreword

*T*he book market is saturated with guides on how to live more successfully. Many require the reader to wade through a myriad of lengthy philosophical beliefs and principles. All too often, well-meaning readers buy these books with every intention of absorbing all the bits of wisdom inside. Unfortunately, many don't have the time to really study such books, let alone extract basic daily living guidelines.

Tom Massey has written a simple book. *The ABC's of Successful Living* cuts to the chase. It is an easy read. Pick it up and you may find yourself motivated to read it from cover to cover at one sitting. Or it may be easier to read whenever you want a spiritual pick-me-up.

This book is a true blessing. In relatively few pages it covers a broad spectrum of practical advice and affirmations for improving your life; for transforming your perspectives on living and being. Use only part of this book and you'll find yourself entering a new level of conscious awareness; use and apply it all and you'll learn that the true secrets of life and universal knowing are essentially simple. This is a very simple book with the power to change your life. It's just that simple.

Arthur B. VanGundy, Ph.D.
Professor of Communication, University of Oklahoma
Author of Brain Boosters for Business Advantage *and* 101 Great Games & Activities *(for corporate trainers), in addition to numerous books on creative thinking and problem solving.*

Contents

1   Affirmations   2

2   Awareness   4

3   Belief   6

4   Bridge Building   8

5   Commitment   10

6   Clean out Your Closets   12

7   Diet   14

8   Divine Intelligence   16

9   Energy of Love   18

10   Enlightenment   20

11   Field Building   22

12   Finances   24

13   Gifts   26

14   Gumption   28

15   Habits   30

16   Humility   32

17   Inclusiveness   34

18   Intuition   36

19   Joyous Giving   38

20   Justice without Judgment   40

21   Keep Your Word   42

22   Know Thyself   44

23   Learn from Your Mistakes   46

24   Love What You Do   48

25	Make Lemons into Lemonade	50
26	Mend Your Fences	52
27	Name It, Then Claim It	54
28	Never Give Up	56
29	Open Your Heart	58
30	Own Your Actions	60
31	Prayer	62
32	Prepare for Opportunity	64
33	Quality of Life	66
34	Quiet Solitude	68
35	Recovery from Stress	70
36	Relationships	72
37	Self-Confidence	74
38	Seize the Day	76
39	Thoughts	78
40	Trust the Process	80
41	Unity Consciousness	82
42	Use Life's Levers	84
43	Validate Those You Appreciate	86
44	Vision	88
45	Wait	90
46	Write Your Own Obituary	92
47	eXpand Your Mental Capacity	94
48	eXpect Change	96
49	Yank Your Own Chain	98
50	Yield to Life's Teaching	100
51	Zeal	102
52	Zone In	104

About this book...

Success is what you define it to be for your life. As the Great Teacher once said, "Where your treasure lies, there lies your heart also." These are some basic principles that will help you create the opportunities for which you dream. Whether success for you is a fulfilling relationship, a career that offers meaningful work and financial rewards, or personal health and well-being, you'll find these words to be beneficial.

This book follows a simple ABC format. Each letter of the alphabet is represented by two words. Each word, 52 in all, is presented as a weekly tip for successful living and achieving a balanced life. Each weekly tip includes a brief narrative, a practical application, and a daily affirmation.

Enjoy!

*T*o laugh often and much;
to win the respect of intelligent people
and affection of children;
to earn the appreciation of honest critics
and endure the betrayal of false friends;
to appreciate beauty,
to find the best in others;
to leave the world a bit better,
whether by a healthy child,
a garden patch
or a redeemed social condition;
to know even one life has breathed easier
because you have lived.
This is to have succeeded.

—Ralph Waldo Emerson

Affirmations

1

Our free-flowing path to *Yes*

*E*verything you want or dream of is trying to happen to you. The *Bhagavad-Gita* (Song of the Lord), the Sanskrit poem that most Hindus regard as the essence of their belief, says, "The winds of God's grace are always blowing. It is we who need to put up our sails."

As you learn to say yes to the blessings that are blowing your way, they will begin to materialize into the physical world. Affirmations have the power to bring profound changes in your life. An affirmation is a positive declaration—stated aloud and in the present tense—that an idea or belief is true. You can affirm the positive qualities about yourself and your life by faith-fully projecting beyond those temporarily limiting circumstances. The magical power of affirmations comes from your own personal belief; you must first *believe* that affirmations work. In *Think and Grow Rich*, best-selling author Napoleon Hill wrote, "Whatever the mind of man can conceive and believe, it can achieve."

Affirmations can also be considered a form of prayer. The purpose of prayer is not to change God, but to change us, aligning our thoughts and actions with God's. As you begin to consistently affirm the Truth of who you are, **your life will miraculously change.**

Application

Choose a daily affirmation about what you would like to manifest into your life and begin with it each day. Repeat the affirmation throughout the day, out loud if possible. The more often you do, the more effective it will be. Let your affirmations represent the truth of your inner being; they should inspire and motivate you when stated.

When you create your own affirmations:

๛* Be personal.

๛* Be positive.

๛* Phrase your affirmation as though it is already in force.

๛* Choose action words.

๛* Be realistic, yet optimistic. Stretch.

For example:

๛* I am an enthusiastic, healthy, radiant person.

๛* I am healthy, strong, and alive.

๛* I capably achieve my goals at the perfect time.

๛* My life is successful and full of wonderful adventures.

๛* Money flows abundantly and freely into my life.

๛* Love surrounds me in all situations.

๛* I am cherished and protected.

Affirmation

I gratefully open my heart, mind, and spirit to receive life's abundant goodness.

Awareness

2

First awaken, then arise

*I*f you asked me for directions to California and I gave you a perfectly good map that charts the route in detail from Texas to California, how would that work for you if your starting point is South Dakota? Probably not too well. An integral part of plotting your journey in life is *knowing where you are now.*

You are accountable for your own life. A common tendency is denial, especially when life is chaotic, painful, or stuck on a detour. There is no awareness in denial. Acknowledge and own where you are today. Your life may be encumbered with adversity that is not your fault, but being a victim is still a matter of personal choice. Job, the biblical sage, who knew adversity well, said, "You will decide on a matter and it will be established for you."

To gain greater awareness, how much better it is to *Name and Claim, without Blame.*

* **Name** the current circumstance your life is in, then
* **claim** responsibility for your part in where you are and where you're headed, but do not
* **blame** yourself or anyone else if life is no bowl of cherries right now.

If you want to undertake positive change in your life, become aware first of where you are, then of where you want to go. Dwight Eisenhower once said, "Change without principle is chaos; change based on principle is progress." Make the changes in your life progressive by using events in the past as lessons for gaining clarity to chart your life course for the future.

If you know where you are, you can find where you're going!

Application

Where are you now? What's working in your life and what isn't? Which personal beliefs limit your growth and success in life? Be completely honest with yourself, as you reflect on your current life circumstances. Don't make excuses and don't lay blame. Simply make adjustments in your life based on what you've learned. If you are willing to acknowledge a circumstance and take ownership of your role in it, you can create the positive change you desire for your life. Begin today!

Affirmation

I am aware of my responsibility for where my life is today and where I am going in the future. Success is mine for the choosing. Naturally, I choose success.

Belief

3

You think you can, you think you can't!
(Either way, you're right!)

*W*hat is belief? Belief is a deliberate activity of consciousness. Belief is a product of thought, and as beings of thought we can change our beliefs. Jesus said, "Go your way; and as you have believed, so let it be done for you" (Matthew 8:13).

If what you believe determines what happens to you, the most important thing for you to do is believe that what happens will be for your utmost benefit—and not just for your highest good, but for the overall highest good of all concerned. Cultivating that "highest" level of belief might sound like a tall order, but you really can't believe just a little bit. Genuine belief is all or nothing, so choose it all. Believe!

Studies of successful people reveal a certain commonality of purpose, based on a strong belief in who they are and what they're doing. Remember, the Great Teacher said that it is done for us, as we believe. If we only believe a little, we get little in return. When we believe much, our rewards are great. The full measure of belief that you put forth will be measured to you in return.

You can do just about anything you think you can. Be bold! Play *big!* In the words of Norman Vincent Peale, "Throw back the shoulders, let the heart sing, let the eyes flash, let the mind be lifted up, look upward and say to yourself . . . **Nothing is impossible!**"

Application

Happiness and success are clearly related to your level of confidence or belief. Abraham Lincoln said, "Most people are about as happy as they make their minds up to be." Have you made your mind up to be happy? What beliefs are defeating you?

Take out a pen and paper and write down your personal beliefs that have been limiting you throughout your life. After you write these down, write a positive affirmation for each belief and repeat those affirmations several times a day, out loud to yourself, for 21 days.

Find at least one other person in your life who wants you to succeed and confess these affirmations to him or her as well. Begin to become aware of the language that you choose to describe yourself and your abilities. Be positive! What you speak will be created and brought forth into the world of form.

Affirmation

I believe that I am blessed with an abundant supply of all things necessary for me to live a happy, successful life.

Bridge Building

Reach, Stretch, Span the gap
from where you are to where you plan to go!

*H*ave you ever thought about all the steps necessary for constructing a bridge? First comes awareness of the need to get from one uncon-nected side to another, then the gathering of resources to construct the bridge that will span this gap. Finally, action will be required to physically build the bridge.

Building bridges to success in your life will require the same process. You must first become aware of the need or desire in your own life to advance from one place to another. Then gather all available resources, beginning with the people in your life who genuinely want to see you suc-ceed. Their knowledge, skills, and support can be very helpful in your endeavor. Some of your own skills may also need honing. Then harness your own emotions to energize you. Your strongest emotions, such as love, passion, and yes, even fear or anger, may become thunderbolts that create a positive "charge" of power to motivate and sustain you.

Finally, take action. Make thoughtful plans and decisions, then pull the trigger: ready, aim, fire! Ultimately the world cares much more about action than thoughts. "Well done is better than well said," as Ben Franklin affirmed. **Life rewards action!**

Application

What bridges need building in your life? The first step is becoming aware of where you are and where you want to go. Once you establish those, make a list of resources you need for constructing your bridge to suc-cess. Who are the people in your life that you can engage to assist you? Some may provide guidance, knowledge, feedback, encouragement, spiritual leadership, or financial support.

What skills do you need to develop to complete this life project? Maybe you need to attend a workshop, read some books, or take some classes to learn the skills you need.

How can you employ every emotion to your benefit? What are you most passionate about? Think about how you can harness the energy of all emotions to create something positive in your life. Visualize what the end result will look like. Then develop a plan and take action a step at a time. Don't count on willpower alone. Set up a system of accountability to keep you on task, with ongoing evaluations that help chart your progress. It's time to step up to the plate in life: you can't get a homerun if you're not swinging!

Affirmation

I am building bridges to success in my life by creating awareness, gathering the resources I need, and employing a plan of action.

Commitment

5

Go for it all!

*I*n 1519 the Spanish conquistador Hernando Cortez led an expedition to Mexico with four hundred men. One night, with the soldiers safely ashore, he burned all their ships so that turning back became impossible. This left nowhere to go but forward. Although outnumbered, they won victory after victory, and his military triumphs led to three hundred years of Spanish dominion over Mexico.

Although you may never lead a military conquest, you may certainly face formidable foes that require you to "burn the ships" so as to ensure total commitment to move forward without retreat. Former college and pro football coach Lou Holtz used to say, "There's no such thing as a ninety percent commitment. You're either committed or you're *not!*"

Highly successful people are totally committed to their life goals and strategies, based on their values. People of commitment have "fire in the belly." They arouse passion within us; they inspire. They engage us and motivate us to "raise the bar" in our own lives.

Are you one of those people who motivate and inspire others to a high level of commitment in their lives? Or are you content to watch from the sidelines, becoming only casually involved when the occasion arises? Consider the analogy of eating ham and eggs for breakfast. The pig was committed to your breakfast, while the chicken was only involved. How about you? **Are you committed, or merely involved?**

Application

Is there an area in your life where you're perched on or straddling the fence? What's keeping you from becoming committed? Is it fear of failure, or fear of success?

F.E.A.R. has been used as an acronym for *False Evidence Appearing Real*. Most of our fears are illusory products of our own perceptions.

Are you involved in a relationship or job in which you are just going through the motions, trying to look busy, when all the while you ache for something better? Did you ever have to make up your mind? When you finally say "yes" to one, you leave the other behind.

An important characteristic of commitment is single-mindedness. Decide what you want and go for it. If you need clarity about what life course to take, sit quietly in a room or in nature and listen. The answer is always within. It's there right now, and it was there all along.

Visualize a picture of the path you should take. Create a daily affirmation and begin to speak it out loud. Profess your commitments to others, as well, to set up personal accountability. If you stumble, hop up and allow those emotions to energize and strengthen you toward an even greater commitment.

Affirmation

I am fully committed to high-level living and excellence. Through my actions I inspire and motivate others to greater commitment in their lives.

Clean out Your Closets 6

Within simplicity lies the sublime!

*H*ave you ever noticed that your life is often a reflection of your closets? The more cluttered your closets are, the messier your life seems to be. Many of us have stored things in our closets for years that we don't need or that no longer serve us. The same is true on an emotional level. We hold onto old, beaten-up emotional baggage that has absolutely no benefit for our lives. In fact, it's a hindrance.

A great spiritual teacher was once asked, "What's the difference between the gurus and the rest of us? Do they have unconditional love and peace in them, and we don't?" His answer: "No. You have peace and unconditional love in you, and so do they. The difference is that they have nothing else inside."

Do you mindlessly store and stockpile old things, rather than actively deciding to either use it or lose it? To hoard is to operate from the fear of scarcity. Is the closet of your life so full of dusty clutter that somewhere deep under the piles of emotional junk you have misplaced your peace of mind? What gain is external, worldly success if the price is to lose your peace? Would success be worth that?

The good news is, you can be successful and have peace of mind, too. Clean out your closets, sweep out all those tangled webs you've been weaving, and **enjoy the life of "simple abundance."**

Application

Set aside some time to **thoughtfully** sort through the mess and clear out your closets. Give away clothes and other things that you haven't used in years. By doing so you will create a space for greater abundance to flow into your life. As you clean out your closets, embrace the symbolism of this act. Begin to mentally go through the closets of your mind and do some cleaning and therapeutic purging there as well. Somewhere underneath the clutter lie the inner peace and contentment that may have been misplaced in your life. These are the raw materials for creativity, the cornerstone of a successful life.

Affirmation

I am creating a life of peace and simple abundance by seeking to keep my closets clear and "current."

Diet

7

Eat to Win!

Several times each day, whether we're aware of it or not, we alter our brain chemistry through what we eat. These changes in brain chemistry cause shifting transformations in moods and mental performance ranging from the subtle to the profound. You have more power than you may have ever realized to shape your inner world. Through smart eating choices you can achieve balanced brain chemistry, resulting in feelings of optimism, confidence, and mental clarity.

Many people in our society reach for drugs when they want to alter their mood. Not only is this unhealthy, it is unnecessary. The greatest manufacturer of drugs is the human brain. And one of the fastest, most powerful ways to produce mood-altering effects is through dietary choices.

Foods cause production shifts within a delicate yet powerful group of chemicals inside the brain called neurotransmitters. These brain chemicals create a wide spectrum of thoughts, feelings, and moods. Your food choices can cause any number of internal states. Foods high in carbohydrates boost levels of serotonin, a neurotransmitter that gives a heightened sense of well-being, a greater ability to concentrate, and more restful sleep.

Diets rich in protein raise levels of dopamine, another important brain chemical that has the opposite effect of serotonin. High levels of dopamine cause states of mental arousal and alertness. Low levels of dopamine can cause depression and disorders of the nervous system, while abnormally high levels may cause anxiety and feelings of aggression or paranoia. Finding the balance between these important brain chemicals is one of the key factors for successful living as you practice the **art of eating for peak performance.**

Application

Start each morning by choosing breakfast foods that are high in protein, such as dairy, poultry, meat, or soy products, to jump-start your mental engine. Add some carbohydrate foods such as grains and fruit to balance the serotonin and dopamine levels that will optimize your mood, energy levels, and ability to concentrate. Repeat this combination for lunch to maintain high productivity and performance throughout the afternoon.

Decrease your protein intake at the evening meal and increase carbohydrate foods, such as pastas, grains, and salads; this will raise your serotonin level to help you relax and get a restful night's sleep.

Affirmation

I am eating for peak performance as I balance my intake of proteins and carbohydrates each day.

Divine Intelligence 8

"You are a distinct portion of the essence of God."

*E*pictetus was an emancipated Greek slave who lived almost two thousand years ago. His words remind us that we contain the essence of the Divine. Imagine the joy of being fully aware that you carry God with you every step of life. Ernest Holmes, who founded the Science of Mind movement in the early 1900s, stated, "We comprehend the meaning of Infinite Intelligence only in a small degree, but because we are spiritual beings, we do sense the presence of an Intelligence which is beyond human comprehension—an Intelligence which is great enough to encompass the past, to understand the present, and to be Father of the future."

Divine Intelligence is the origin of everything. It is God in whom we live, and move, and have our being. In an ancient Sanskrit saying, "God sleeps in the minerals, awakens in the plants, walks in the animals, and thinks in you."

Use this presence of the Divine to realize the magnitude of your thinking capacity. Ultimately it will not be people, circumstances, or events that determine your success. That will be determined by your realization that you have an invisible source, Divine Intelligence, which will equip you with all that you need.

Let go of any inclination to compare yourself to others or to blame external circumstances for your unhappiness. Rather, remind yourself daily that you share the mind of the Divine Creator and **you are a divine creation.**

Application
Practice daily rituals that affirm the presence of the Divine in you and all that you do. Give thanks for everything you receive, including your food, shelter, air that you breathe, sunshine, rain, and so forth. Gratitude is one

of the best ways to acknowledge and recognize God in all things. Visualize daily the energy of Divine Intelligence in every cell of your being. Know that it is there to bring peace, happiness, and perfect health.

Affirmation

I am thankful for God's presence that exists within me, and open to receiving the blessings of abundance in my life.

Energy of Love

9

May the Force be with you!

*A*lbert Einstein once said, "One cannot help but be in awe when he contemplates the mysteries of eternity, of life, of the marvelous structure of reality." Within each cell of our human bodies are trillions of infinitesimal atoms and subatomic particles. When a given number of electrons are aligned within one atom contained in one molecule, a force of energy is produced.

Energy movement within the billions of cells in our body is completely orchestrated by the power of our minds, which is connected to a vast Universal Energy. We orchestrate energy first with our thoughts; thus the proverb, "As a man thinks, so he is." Thoughts are like seeds, planted in soil and left to grow. The fruit that grows is always the essence of what was planted. By the Farmer's Law, "If you plant potatoes, you'll reap potatoes."

Thought produces language, which also orchestrates energy. When you are speaking words, especially about yourself to yourself, your cells stand up and listen, just like in the E. F. Hutton commercial.

"*I am*" are the most powerful words in our language. When you say words like, "I am a success!" or "I am brilliant!" you create a very different energy (Farmer's Law, again) than if you were to say, "I am a failure!" or "I am stupid." That's the reason positive affirmations are so powerful.

Energy is also orchestrated by emotions. Strong negative emotions, such as anger and fear, create a powerful energy very different from that created by emotions such as love. The power of love is the most powerful of all energies because it not only spans our own thoughts, language, and emotions, but also bridges the gap between us and everything else in existence. Love is the sustaining life energy and the glue that holds the world together. Poet Robert Browning said, "Take away love, and our earth is a tomb."

We have only begun to realize the magnitude of love's power. In the words of French-born philosopher Pierre Teilhard de Chardin, "Someday, after we have mastered the winds, the waves, the tide and gravity, we shall harness for God the energies of love. Then, for the second time in the history of the world, man will have discovered fire."

Your success depends entirely upon pursuing what you love. That love will keep you alive! **Seek love's energy as if your life depended on it, because it does.**

Application

Every thought you have, every word you speak, every emotion you feel, and every action you take on behalf of love moves you closer to discovering fire for the second time. Let go of any negative thoughts by first becoming aware of them when they enter your consciousness. Then, as Wayne Dyer says, simply tell yourself, "Next thought."

Rather than verbally criticizing yourself or others because of failures, let go of expectations and silently project love. As you do this, you will begin to experience the same response coming back to you from the world in which you live. You will attract back into your life what you send out. If you plant seeds of love, peace, and acceptance, you'll reap the same. You take what you make.

Affirmation

I am a powerful, loving being who allows the energy of love to flow freely in and out of my life.

Enlightenment

After the Ecstasy, the Laundry

*I*n Jack Kornfeld's beautifully written book, *After the Ecstasy, the Laundry*, the author assures us, "Enlightenment does exist. . . . It is possible to awaken. Unbounded freedom and joy, oneness with the Divine, awakening into a state of timeless grace . . . these experiences are more common than you know, and not far away. There is one further truth, however: They don't last."

After rising to higher consciousness on the wings of enlightenment, we are still faced with doing the laundry and other mundane, day-to-day tasks of transferring that freedom into our imperfect lives. As the well-worn Zen proverb says, "Before enlightenment, chopping wood, carrying water. After enlightenment, chopping wood, carrying water."

The message here is that enlightenment is not an attainment, but a realization that everything appears to have changed, and yet no change has taken place. *You simply begin to see the world through different eyes.* Enlightenment does not begin with a vision quest or a pilgrimage to the holy land. It is not something you will obtain from a guru, a book, or a weekend workshop. Enlightenment is an attitude toward everything you do, whether chopping wood, carrying water, doing the laundry, or gazing into the eyes of a lover.

The Buddhists say, "Keep a beginner's mind." Have you ever really watched a small child play? They move about with great wonder of every moment that transpires in their life. If we are to maintain an enlightened state we must do the same. You will have times when those mountaintop experiences begin to wane. Don't become discouraged in the valleys of life; even the greatest mystics have experienced the "dark night of the soul."

Consider those moments to be a birthing process. Birthing may be painful, but it brings forth new life. Enlightenment is a state of being "born again" into that state of "everything has changed, but nothing's changed." Each day you are born again. And every day you have a fresh start in life. **Success lies in the newness of life!**

Application

Let go of your belief that enlightenment is something you will achieve at some point in the future when your life circumstances change for the better. You will always have some form of chopping wood, carrying water, or doing laundry in your life. It is your choice about how you elect to see it. Practice with specific affirmations that in all situations you choose peace. When you're in a traffic jam or a long line, keep repeating to yourself, "I choose peace in this moment." Use the ordinary circumstances of life for practicing shifts in your inner world. *Reserve a space within you for rest*—an internal place to which you can retreat in moments of anguish or despair. Finally, walk in a spirit of humility. The person who is enlightened never boasts of it. The person who says, "I'm enlightened," is most assuredly not.

Affirmation

I embrace enlightenment by approaching each day with childlike wonder and appreciation for life.

Field Building

11

If you build it, they will come.

*T*he 1989 blockbuster *Field of Dreams* is a movie whose story and setting continue to inspire. Created for the film on a farm in Dyersville, Iowa, the mystical cornfield and magnificent baseball field still glisten, to this day, in the morning sun. The field remains, continuing to draw millions of tourists, worldwide: *seekers who want to believe.*

People are magically drawn to this place, to this space, for reasons they can't explain. It exudes everything that is wonderful with its relaxed pace, pristine setting and rich history, inspiring each visitor to supply whatever drama he or she desires. True to the simplicity and immaculate quality that made the film so powerful and endearing, the Field of Dreams Movie Site and all who visit benefit by the property remaining as a magnetic, green and growing beacon of hope.

Kevin Costner's character was a struggling farmer named Ray Kinsella who kept hearing a voice whispering, "If you build it, they will come." No one believed him initially, except his wife. Despite objections and ridicule from neighbors and an ever-widening circle of detractors, Ray plowed under a good crop to build a baseball field. As a reward for their unwavering conviction, Mr. and Mrs. Kinsella both encountered the "ghost players" who arrived at their heaven-on-earth for a game of baseball.

Success will come to you when you commit to doing your own field building. Listen to the quiet, confident voice within, believe in yourself, and pursue your dreams, regardless of what others may think. **You'll see it when you build it!**

Application

What fields are you building? Are you looking for the right partner to have a wonderful relationship with and make your life complete? Then

The ABC's of Successful Living

work on becoming the right partner by building a balanced life of wholeness and personal contentment. If you do this, you won't have to worry about *finding* the right partner. The right partner will show up in your life.

Perhaps you're looking for that perfect job or career. What are you doing to prepare for it? Are you field-building by developing skills and nurturing relationships that can help create meaningful, rewarding work for you? Work on sharpening your saw daily in preparation for the opportunities that inevitably come your way. Life is full of rewards for field builders.

Affirmation

I am field-building in all areas, and wonderful relationships and opportunities are coming into my life.

Finances

12

The worthiest investment is *you!*

*R*obert Kiyosaki, author of *Rich Dad Poor Dad,* says, "The main reason people struggle financially is because they have spent years in school but learned nothing about money. People learn to work for money . . . but never learn to have money work for them." He explains that the key to financial freedom is a person's ability to convert earned income into passive income and/or portfolio income. If you are like many Americans, by the time Uncle Sam gets paid you have managed to spend every remaining cent—at least! From a self-imposed position of weakness, you are not in a position to consider the concept of passive or portfolio income.

The first secret is to "fatten your purse." In George Clason's book, *The Richest Man in Babylon,* the wealthy Arkad asks a humble egg merchant, "If thou select one of thy baskets and put into it each morning ten eggs and take out from it each evening nine eggs, what will eventually happen?" The merchant said, "It will become in time overflowing, because each day I put in one more egg than I take out."

To bring your dreams and desires to fruition, you must invest in *you.* The first law of gold, Clason says, is, "Gold cometh gladly and in increasing quantity to any man who will put by not less than one-tenth of his earnings to create an estate for his future and that of his family."

The message is clear: to be financially successful, you must set aside a portion of your earnings for *you.* You are the goose that's laying *your* golden eggs. Reward yourself and dispel any limiting beliefs, such as "The love of money is the root of all evil," by repeated affirmations that you are a child of an Abundant God who has granted an infinite inheritance for all that you will ever need. **The Universe knows no scarcity.**

The ABC's of Successful Living

Application

You can create positive change for financial success in your life by following three simple, yet profound principles:

- ⚜ **Live by the 80/20 rule.** Set aside the first 10% of what you make to give in gratitude back to God, the Universe, or whatever you call the Giver of all things. Set aside the second 10% as an investment in yourself and your family. Then learn to live on the other 80%.

- ⚜ **Stay out of debt.** The grips of debt can be strangulating. Debt eats away at the heart of your financial resources. Tear up your credit cards and their exorbitant interest rates and learn to live on what you make in the present.

- ⚜ **Do what you love and the financial success will come.** When you're in love with what you do, that love is contagious. It infects everyone around you in positive ways that will create opportunities beyond your wildest dreams.

Affirmation

I enjoy abundant financial success from doing work that I love.

Gifts

13

Use them or lose them!

Jesus told the parable of a rich man who was leaving on an extended trip. He called his servants together and delegated responsibilities. To one man he gave five thousand dollars, to another he gave two thousand, and to a third the rich man gave one thousand dollars. To each he gave according to his abilities. Then he left. Immediately the first man went to work and doubled his master's investment. The second did the same. But the man with the one thousand dollars dug a hole and buried it for safe-keeping.

After a long absence the rich man returned and asked his servants to settle up. To each man who doubled his investment he said, "Congratulations on a job well done! From now on I want you to be my partner." The third man offered up several excuses. He was afraid that his master had such high standards and would demand the best, allowing no room for error. And he was afraid he might disappoint his master, so he secured a good hiding place to keep the money safe and sound. The rich man was furious. "That's a terrible way to live," he said. "It's criminal to live so cautiously!" The man was admonished for making no effort to at least produce a minimal interest on his master's investment. The rich man then made him give his thousand dollars to the man who had risked the most, and the cautious man was cast in prison for his "play-it-safe" attitude.

Within this parable lies a great secret to successful living. The money represents gifts or talents that we are given by the Creator. It is up to us to use our talents according to our abilities. If we are faithful in using these talents, we are rewarded with additional gifts, as well as partnership with the Source of overflowing abundance. If we choose to let our fears keep us from using our talents, we not only lose them, but also become imprisoned by our fears in the process.

Are you using your talents in life? Or are you keeping them buried somewhere in a hole of fear? What are you afraid of? **Playing it safe presents the greatest risk.**

Application

You will be most fulfilled and at your best when using your natural gifts in a purposeful way. George Bernard Shaw said, "This is the true joy—the being used for a purpose recognized as a mighty one." What gifts have you been given? What are the things that really get your juices flowing and adrenaline pumping? Are you investing your time into them and developing other talents in the process? Sit down and make an inventory of your special abilities. You may want to engage your mate or a close friend who may give you additional insight. Perhaps you have the talent of speaking, or teaching, or writing, or singing, or playing a musical instrument, or working with your hands as a technician, a mechanic, or carpenter, or creating art or sculpting. Perhaps your greatest gifts are of service, or mercy, or giving, or encouraging others. Whatever your gifts may be, make a commitment to use them and develop others as well. Because of changing demands in today's world, those who diversify their skills will experience the greatest success.

Affirmation

I am using and multiplying my talents as I experience rewards and a partnership of abundance with the Creator.

Gumption

14

Ask for what you want!

*P*eople of powerful vision and total commitment to accomplishing their goals all have one characteristic in common: They know how to ask for what they want. For them, asking with passion is a natural way to make continuous progress on the path to success. Asking is a catalyst for change. Martin Luther King, Jr., changed the course of our country's history because he asked people to share his dream of equality for all people. Mahatmas Gandhi changed the course of his nation by asking his countrymen to join him in peaceful revolution to win autonomy for India. Winston Churchill asked the people of Great Britain to "never, never, never, never give up," and the country was saved from a Nazi invasion.

Each day presents many golden opportunities to ask for what you want. Pay attention to those moments and step forward boldly to make your requests known. Don't ever assume that people know what you want or need. It is *your* responsibility to make this known. The Scriptures say, "You have not, because *you* ask not."

By asking today for what you want, you will plant the seeds that will enable you to enjoy tomorrow's harvest of success and prosperity. Let go of the belief that asking reveals weaknesses in your armor. We all, at times, need assistance from others. There is no shame in asking or admitting that we're not in this alone. If it was good enough for King, Gandhi, and Churchill, it's good enough for you. As seventeenth-century poet John Donne said, "No man is an island, entire of itself; every man is a piece of the continent, a part of the main." **Ask and you shall receive!**

Application

Are you enjoying the fruits of asking? The following steps will help you move closer to getting what you want through the art of effective asking:

- **Ask with laser-like clarity.** Ask yourself, "What do I really want?" Make a list of your wants in life and prioritize your list according to the importance of each item. Go after the most important ones first. Once you decide what you really want, take time to prepare your requests to others. Be specific and ask precisely for what *you* want.
- **Ask with confidence.** People who are confident get more out of life than those who are hesitant or filled with self-doubt. Asking with boldness and confidence does not in any way make you arrogant or conceited. Rather, you will possess a quiet strength that people will sense and be drawn towards.
- **Ask consistently.** Don't fold up your tent after one timid request. Most successful sales people will tell you that asking is like a numbers game. Most people have to go through four or five *nos* to get to a *yes*. As you practice asking you will become more skillful in unearthing the true riches in life.
- **Ask with sincerity and gratitude.** When you ask in a spirit of sincerity and an attitude of gratitude, people will respond. Your willingness to be real and vulnerable will touch the hearts of those you ask. Simply tell it the way it is.

Affirmation

I am receiving the things I want in life by asking with clarity, specificity, consistency, sincerity, and gratitude.

Habits

15

If you keep on doing what you've always done, you'll keep on getting what you've always gotten.

Your habits play a major role in how your future unfolds. Life never just happens. Instead it is a daily process of making choices and responding to every situation. If you are in the habit of continually making wise choices, then success is likely to occur. Successful people have successful habits.

What is a habit? Simply stated, a habit is a behavior that you repeat so often that it becomes easy. The key to developing a habit is persistence. If you persist at developing any new behavior, it eventually becomes automatic. Many people today are looking for a more fulfilling life. Material prosperity is only part of living successfully. Creating meaningful relationships, enriching your health, enjoying a balance between work and play, and nourishing your own spirit and soul are all ingredients in the recipe for quality living.

Successful people don't accidentally drift to the top of the heap in life. They stay focused, disciplined, and committed each day to expend the energy to make things happen. Whether you are rich or poor, healthy or unhealthy, fulfilled or unfulfilled, you are experiencing a series of consequences based on your repeated thoughts and behavior. Life always yields consequences, which you may like or dislike. You have the ability to turn the undesirable consequences of tomorrow into rewarding results simply by changing your habits today. **Successful habits create positive outcomes.**

Application

How long does it take to develop a habit? Depending on the behavior study you peruse, anywhere between twenty-one and thirty days. What's amazing is that after twenty-one to thirty experiences with a new behavior, it becomes harder *not* to do it than to do it. It's similar to building a rope. Every time you repeat the behavior you add another strand, making the rope stronger and stronger.

When changing a habit, first check how long you have owned it. If you have been doing something over twenty years, you may not be able to let go of it in a few weeks. For people such as long-time smokers or those with a long history of low self-esteem, it may take a year or more. Some ropes take a long time to unravel. But as you unravel the rope of the old habit, add strands to a new rope of a habit that serves you better. The transformation will affect both your personal and professional life.

If other people have made significant changes in habits, so can you. But remember, nothing will change until *you* do. Embrace the changes within you as a positive catalyst that will produce a sense of peace and fulfillment.

Affirmation

I am weaving many strands into habits that bring love and peace to everyone in my life.

Humility

16

There's no limit to the amount of good we can accomplish, if we don't care who gets the credit.

In his book, *Wisdom of the Ages,* Wayne Dyer writes, "For me, the measure of greatness and happiness is the ability to subjugate ego to the point of needing no credit for accomplishments, to be beyond needing gratitude or applause, to be independent of the good opinion of others, to just be doing what I do, because it is my purpose to do so."

Humility is about being focused and living purposefully, free of the need to be noticed. Oliver Wendell Holmes once said, "With all humility, I think, 'Whatsoever thy hand findeth to do, do it with thy might.' Infinitely more important than the vain attempt to love one's neighbor as one's self. If you want to hit a bird on the wing, you must have all your will in focus, you must not be thinking about yourself, and equally, you must not be thinking about your neighbor: you must be living in your eye on that bird. Every achievement is a bird on the wing."

Humility is not about being a doormat, or timid, or weak. Rather it is about the "least shall be the greatest" principle that Jesus taught. There is strength in humility. The great teachers of the world have all possessed this gentle strength. They are ordinary beings, yet extraordinarily powerful in simple ways. Lao-tzu reminded us, "All streams flow to the ocean because it is lower than they are. Humility gives it its power."

Humility is being the best you can be. It is working from the heart with the Creator, in understanding and knowing the true meaning of beauty. It allows us to open our hearts and minds to the full realization of the sacredness of Life. And as Thoreau said, **"Humility, like darkness, reveals the heavenly lights."**

Application

Practice "random acts of kindness, and senseless acts of beauty." Give anonymously to anyone in need, without asking for or expecting recognition or praise in return. Rejuvenate yourself with moments of solitude in nature. Be still and listen to the sounds of the wind, the waves breaking on the surf, or the calls of the birds and other animals. As you quietly breathe in the fresh air, open your heart and mind to the beauty that surrounds you and drink in the presence of the Divine.

Affirmation

I am humbly, yet powerfully, opening my heart and mind to the beauty around me.

Inclusiveness

17

There is unity in diversity.

*I*f you look at coins minted in the U.S., you will see the Latin words, *e pluribus unum,* which means, "unity in diversity." Our founding fathers shared a philosophy of inclusion with all the deep thinkers of the ages. This is a simple and direct approach that causes us to experience oneness with creation, with each other, and with all human events. Our willingness to embrace diversity is one of the factors that have molded America into one of the greatest nations in the history of the planet. Nineteenth-century poet Emma Lazarus penned these words, which were later inscribed on the Statue of Liberty:

> Give me your tired, your poor,
> Your huddled masses yearning to breathe free,
> The wretched refuse of your teeming shore.
> Send these, the homeless, tempest-tost to me,
> I lift my lamp beside the golden door!

We are all unique in some way. In many ways our ideals may seem opposite from those of others we meet. But that seeming opposition may turn out to be complementary ideals that add up to much more than the sum of their parts. They may complement each other like night and day, male and female, or yin and yang. The complementary nature of opposites is apparent even in the field of science. Physicist Emilio Segre wrote, "It is one of the special beauties of science that points of view which seem diametrically opposed turn out later, in a broader perspective, to be both right."

Spiritual maturity is the zenith of successful living. And the truest mark of spiritual maturity is the willingness to accept another's sense of the truth without it invalidating your own, no matter how contradictory it appears. Regardless of our differences, we all belong to the family of humanity. The Native Americans have an expression that describes this connectedness. It is *Mitakuye oyasin*, which can be translated as, **"We're all related."**

Application

Do you ever feel disconnected from others because of differences? Maybe their skin is a different color, or they have a different political persuasion, or perhaps they call God by a different name than you. Make a commitment for today to suspend all judgment and simply love people for who they are. Mother Teresa once said that she saw Christ in the face of every person she helped. Let go of your need to be right and accept all people as physical manifestations of the Divine. Then you will truly feel the bliss of these beautifully expressed words, "Today I touch the Face of God, and meet you there."

Affirmation

I embrace the Divineness in every person I meet and fully appreciate the unity in our diversity.

Intuition

18

Listen to the voice within.

*I*ntuition is a powerful word because it means so many different things to different people. According to the *Random House Dictionary*, intuition is "direct perception of truth, fact, etc., independent of any reasoning process." In simple words, it is a "knowing without knowing how you know." Intuition has also been defined by some scientists as the brain's capacity for subliminal computation, while others believe that it is predicated by biological instinct, learned habits, or social conditioning. The fabric of intuition may well include all these threads as well as others.

It is through intuition that we construct and maintain our sense of space and time, our sense of identity, our sense of truth, and our sense of beauty. All of our sensory perceptions and rational thoughts would scatter like cards in the wind were it not for the glue of intuition holding the house of our lives together. Intuition is a delicate sensitivity, within our deepest being, to the pulses of life's energies.

Successful people learn to listen to the quiet whisper of their intuitive voice. That voice is an internal compass that sets the direction of the life journey. Sometimes it is a hunch about something that is going to happen or an overwhelming feeling about a certain situation. Other times intuition may come in the form of a deep inner restlessness. Ralph Waldo Emerson called this restlessness "divine discontent." It is divine because it could be God who is stirring those feelings inside you. The voice of intuition is not nagging or tiresome; rather, it is a persistent, loving nudge that guides you to awaken to the truest desires of your heart. Do you have a restlessness, a divine discontent, welling up inside your soul? Listen to your intuitive voice and respect that feeling that nudges you toward higher living. It might be God's voice saying, **"Don't settle for less, there's much more for you."**

Application

Where is the voice of intuition leading you? What is the deepest longing of your heart? What are your "gut feelings" about where you're headed in life? Sit with a partner and share those feelings. Share your dreams and most heartfelt desires. Some of the greatest ideas have been given birth by people who heeded the message of their hearts and were willing to risk exploring new possibilities together. Sit quietly and listen to the still small voice within. You contain much more than you know. Your Creator has endowed you with an unlimited potential for expression. As you awaken and listen to the voice of intuition brought forth by your heart's deepest longings, you will get into touch with dormant powers that will empower you with an energy to create a life beyond your wildest dreams.

Affirmation

I am experiencing success and abundance each day by listening to and honoring the voice of intuition that flows from my deepest heart's desires.

Joyous Giving   *19*

Give, and it shall be given unto you!

*J*esus was very specific in his teaching about the law of giving: "Give, and it will be given to you: good measure, pressed down, shaken together, and running over will be put into your bosom. For with the same measure that you use, it will be measured back to you" (Luke 6:38).

Giving is a fundamental spiritual law. Just as you cannot live without breathing, you cannot live to your fullest potential without giving. Through giving you become a channel through which abundance flows in and out of your life. Having an abundant life means fully experiencing love and peace in all areas of your life—your health, relationships, and finances.

Giving has nothing to do with what you have; rather, it has everything to do with who you are being. Are you being joyful and generous? When you give joyously and generously, without thoughts of getting anything in return, the windows of prosperity open to you and pour out blessings into your lap. By infusing the energy of joyous giving into your life, you'll open doors to a limitless supply of creativity, opportunities, personal fulfillment and material abundance. Successful living and abundance evolve through giving. Are you willing to be prosperous? "Prove me now," God says in the Old Testament. **Give, and you will receive!**

Application

Think of your work as giving. Look at each relationship—your family, your friends, strangers you meet on the street—as an opportunity to give. Develop the practice of giving without worrying what you'll receive in return. Recognize that you have one Source of abundance that may flow to you through many channels. Your job, your skills, and your bank account are not your sources. They are merely channels. When you truly align yourself with your Infinite Source of abundance, you will remain prosperous regardless of your present circumstances. Begin to circulate the flow of energy in and out of your life by giving your time, talents, and what you treasure. Think "give."

Affirmation

I joyously give to others from the limitless supply of abundance that flows freely to me from the Divine Infinite Source of all things.

Justice without Judgment 20

Dress your love in work clothes!

*R*emember the biblical story of the prodigal son who had lost everything he possessed in a far country. After becoming sick and discouraged, he returned to his father's house, where he was welcomed with open arms. His father didn't judge or condemn him, nor did he even ask where his son had been or what he had been doing. Instead the father simply proclaimed, "Let us rejoice together."

We all know what the fear of rejection or punishment can produce in our lives. It can shrivel hopes and dreams. It can close down avenues of self-expression and creativity. It can dampen the ardor of living and reduce one to a physical or mental wreck. In these moments we become, like the prodigal son, sick and discouraged, alone in the far country of disillusionment. If we but knew how welcomed we would be, we would return and rejoice in the warmth of our Father's house.

Justice appears in the world through the process of cause and effect, not by the action of a Divine Judge intent on punishing us for the mistakes we make. We are not punished *for* our mistakes, but *by* them. Each of us must assume responsibility for his own actions. Every thought and every action produces consequences. You have the power to change the consequences you are experiencing by changing your thoughts and actions. Like the prodigal son, you've probably made some huge mistakes in the past. Don't perpetuate those by continuing to live in the far country of poverty and despair. Instead, return home to the embracing arms of love and forgiveness.

Each moment of life is a gift. How often we forget this and spend precious time regretting or beating ourselves up over things we've done in the past. The only time you can do anything about is *now*, and in this present moment you are free to suspend all judgment about the past. **Choose to love yourself and others unconditionally, leaving fear and judgment behind.**

Application

Life is an exciting adventure in which we never know what lies beyond the turn in the road. But too often our thoughts today are filled with regrets of yesterday. If we could but convince ourselves that we need not carry the past with us, what a happy outlook we would have. Today is the time to cut loose from the threads of previous experiences, and deliberately make up your mind to live each day as though it were complete and perfect within itself. Life is made to be lived successfully and joyfully. Accept this and repeat daily affirmations that reinforce it in your consciousness. Loosen the bonds of judgment by forgiving yourself and others for everything that has happened up until now. As you disconnect from the past and firmly root the present in love, hope, joyful expectancy, and gratitude, you will learn to live in harmony with everything that transpires today, and tomorrow will blossom like a new flower in the garden of your experience.

Affirmation

I deliberately choose to let go of the past and live in peace, harmony, and love in the present.

Keep Your Word

21

The Truth will set you free!

*I*n the beautifully written book, *The Four Agreements*, Don Miguel Ruiz reveals a powerful code of conduct that can transform our lives into a new experience of personal freedom and happiness. The first agreement, which Ruiz says is the cornerstone of that personal transformation, is to *be impeccable with your word*. Why your word? Because your word is the most powerful tool you have for creating what you want.

The New Testament Gospel of John says, "In the beginning was the Word, and the Word was with God, and the Word was God." Being made in the image of God, we are given the power through our spoken word to manifest what we want. Ruiz calls words "the tools of magic."

When you are impeccable with your word, you feel happy and at peace. That is what is meant by "the truth shall set you free." Keeping your word garners a sense of trust in all relationships you develop. It especially helps you develop a heightened sense of self-trust and an image of high self-worth. Alexander Pope said, "An honest man is the noblest work of God."

Highly successful people establish personal credibility through keeping their word. If they make promises, they make every effort to keep them. If you want to experience success in your life, whether in your relationships or your work, it is imperative that you keep your word. Will you always be able to keep it? Probably not, but you can *always do your best*. That is one of Ruiz's four agreements, too. Make an agreement with yourself today to **be impeccable with your word!**

Application

What do people say about your word? Is it impeccable? Are you a promise-keeper? Honesty must start with you. Are you honest with yourself? When you truly commit to keeping your word you will begin to see exciting new changes happening in your life. First you will see changes in the way you deal with yourself. How you feel about yourself is directly proportionate to the integrity of your word. Second, you will experience changes in your relationships as they become more open and loving. Third, you will reap tremendous gains in success and abundance in your work by developing a reputation of impeccability. This does not mean that you can do or be all things to all people. Learn that "No." is a complete sentence. It is better to give an honest "no" than to say "yes" and not keep your word. Simplify your life and experience personal freedom by speaking the truth in love.

Affirmation

*I am impeccable with my word as I experience love,
happiness, and success in all my relationships and work.*

Know Thyself 22

"For in thyself is found *all* there is to be known."

*I*n each of us there is a natural potential for harmony, beauty, and perfect well-being. This potential is not found in our intellect, or our body of flesh and bones. It is found in the energies of our Soul and Self, which sustain our human form, giving rise to our inherent powers of thought, feeling, and action. The knowledge of these energies opens the way for inner peace, balance, and harmony in the totality of our being.

It was Socrates who told us that "the unexamined life is not worth living, that to know one's self is the primary goal of the thinking person." Lao Tzu believed that the best way to know your enemy is to know yourself. The starting point in developing your personal journey and overcoming any obstacles to success is to understand your personality, talents, dreams, and desires, and to develop a strategy to optimize their harmonized unfolding.

According to the Greeks, the essence of all teaching lies in the phrase, *Know thyself.* "Let him who would move the world, first move himself," said Socrates. Every person and thing you see in the world is a mirror reflecting back to you that which you perceive to be real. Each time a situation arises in your life that rocks your boat or pushes your buttons, ask yourself, "What is it in me that is creating this reality?" The answer is within you: "For in thyself is found *all* there is to be known."

"Knowledge is the wing whereby we fly to Heaven," said Shakespeare. As you undertake your own journey toward self-discovery, you will open doors to inner peace and bliss. **Heaven is within you!**

Application
You can gain greater awareness and self-knowledge in a variety of ways. One way is to record your thoughts each day in a journal. Another is to

make a list of your core life values, then go back and reflect on where each of those values came from. Ask your mate or a close friend to describe your essence to you. Have them write down all the qualities they perceive in you.

Another good tool for enhancing your self-knowledge is psychological testing. The Internet has numerous web sites that offer free personality, learning styles, intelligence, and scholastic aptitude tests. Many of these sites offer excellent interpretations of the test results. The better you know yourself, the more focused, purposeful, and successful you will be.

Affirmation

I have the power to create happiness, success, and well-being in my life by deepening my self-knowledge and personal awareness.

Learn from Your Mistakes

23

Success is on the far side of failure!

Soichiro Honda was still in school in 1938 when Japan, like most other countries, was hit badly by the Great Depression of the 1930s. He labored day and night to develop a piston ring that he hoped to sell to Toyota. He even pawned his wife's jewelry to get working capital to finance his dream. After finally completing his piston ring and delivering it to Toyota, he was ridiculed by the engineers, who laughed at his design.

Soichiro refused to give up. Rather than focusing on his failure, he continued working toward his goal. After two more years of struggle and redesign he won a contract with Toyota. Throughout the following years, he experienced one setback after another, including having his factory destroyed by an earthquake and by bombs during the war. Each time, he learned from his mistakes and continued building his dream.

Today, Honda Corporation employs over 100,000 people in the USA and Japan, and is one of the world's largest automobile companies. Honda succeeded because one man truly committed to a decision, acted upon it, learned from his mistakes, and made adjustments on a continual basis.

Other great pioneers in the fields of science and medicine have modeled the same dedication in learning from their mistakes. Thomas Edison made hundreds of attempts before perfecting the light bulb. Dr. Jonas Salk tried hundreds of formulas before he discovered the polio vaccine. Giving up was simply not an option for these men. Learn from them, and don't let mistakes foil your dreams, either. Stay energized, and with each setback become more determined to achieve what you aspire to. Remember these words by Soichiro Honda, **"Success is ninety-nine percent failure!"**

Application

Has fear of failure paralyzed you and kept you from achieving success in your life? Do people laugh at you or ridicule you when you express innovative ideas or goals? Don't be surprised when this happens. Most of the great minds throughout history have been laughed at and ridiculed. Einstein said, "Geniuses are often met with violent opposition by those with mediocre minds." Start thinking "outside the box" and expand your way of looking at life. Daydream and ponder what might be. Act upon your dreams and aspirations, regardless of what the naysayers in your life tell you. As Wayne Dyer says, "Become independent of the good opinion of others," and march to the beat of your own drum. You cannot fail unless you quit!

Affirmation

I learn from each mistake and am totally committed to acting upon my dreams and aspirations.

Love What You Do 24

...and you'll never have to work!

*M*any of us were raised to believe that it is the "norm" to lead two lives: one from nine to five, and the other in the hours afterwards—our "real lives." Like our parents before us, we divide our lives between what we have to do and what we want to do. Many college students today study for degrees they don't care about, in order to land jobs they don't want. How depressing to think that these people would spend so many years becoming educated, just to get a job in which they spend much of their time "passing time."

It's true that everyone needs to make a living, and people choose jobs for various reasons: financial stability, security, respect, etc. But if you choose a career only because of the money, you have become a part of one of the oldest professions: you are prostituting yourself. Is the annual vacation to Disneyland worth that?

The good news is that there is a better way to live. We currently have more options and opportunities available to us than at any other time in history. Do what you love and the money will come. Author and financial consultant Suze Orman says one of the steps to financial freedom is, "Learn to recognize true wealth. Money itself will not make you financially free. That comes as a result of only that powerful state of mind which tells us that we are worth far more than our money."

The fact is most people will continue to work for money rather than love, but you can choose to live differently. Why do what most people can or will do, when you can do what most people can't or won't? For what should your work profit you?

Do it for love!

Application

Life is precious; spend it doing something you love. You'll spend about as much time on your job as you do with your mate. You can make both a happier marriage by making one of two choices: (1) Do what you love, or (2) learn to love what you do. Often it will be a process of doing the latter until you can position yourself to do the former. If you want to do what you love, first you have to decide what that might be. Think about and write down the three things you most like to do in life (eating and sex don't count). What are the things that arouse the greatest amount of passion in you? Think back in your life to those ecstatic moments where time stood still for you. Somewhere in those moments lies a vocation that can be fulfilling and purposeful for you.

Don't be afraid to seek the help of a career counselor or friend who can help you identify potential areas that are suited to your natural talents. After you identify what you want, develop a plan or strategy to get where you want to go. You may need to go to school or take classes to develop additional skills. You may need to ask help from someone in the career field you want to enter. Wherever your love takes you, connect with the resources that will help you build your bridge to success.

Affirmation

My life is full of passion and purpose as I do what I love and love what I do.

Make Lemons into Lemonade

25

Create your own silver lining in the clouds!

*D*uring the 1960 Rome Olympics, Wilma Rudolph became the fastest woman in the world and the first American woman to win three gold medals in one Olympics. She won the 100- and 200-meter races and anchored the U.S. team to victory in the 4 x 100-meter relay, breaking world records along the way.

Those were fantastic feats, but becoming the world's fastest female wasn't the greatest challenge that Wilma Rudolph beat. As a child, the seventeenth of twenty-one children, she was afflicted with polio, scarlet fever, and double pneumonia. She grew up wearing a brace on her right leg and sneaked behind her parents back to learn to walk on her own. To her doctor's astonishment, Wilma removed the brace and walked unassisted by age nine. She didn't stop there. By age thirteen, Wilma was outracing all the neighborhood kids, and by fourteen she qualified for the 1956 Olympics, where she won a bronze medal in the 4 x 100-meter relay.

Throughout her life, Wilma never backed away from a challenge or a cause. As an African American, she participated in peaceful demonstrations at businesses that were open to whites only. She opened and ran a community center for underprivileged children and established the Wilma Rudolph Foundation, which supplies schools with tutors and books about American heroes. Wilma was indeed a great American hero. With her courage, determination to succeed, and faith in God, she turned a passel of lemons into lemonade.

We can all learn lessons from heroes like Wilma Rudolph. Life is what you make it. Whether you think you can or you think you can't, you'll probably prove yourself right. When life hands you lemons, what you do with them is your choice. You can pucker up, make a face, and feel sorry for yourself. Or do like Wilma and squeeze every drop out of them and make yourself some fresh lemonade. **How sweet it is!**

Application

Unless you've lived inside a bubble, you have likely tasted some lemons in your life. You may not have experienced polio, scarlet fever, and double pneumonia, but as Gilda Radner said, "It's always something" happening in our lives that ruffles our feathers. How have you responded, up until now, to these moments in your life? Have you seen them as opportunities to "raise the bar" in your life? Have you allowed the energy of fear, anger, and frustration to propel you to greater feats? Or are you holding a grudge against someone or something in life that gave you a sour deal? Holding a grudge only hurts you. It's like taking poison and expecting someone else to die. Someone once said, "Don't get mad, get even." The best way to get even is to turn lemons into lemonade. Living a good life is the sweetest revenge!

Affirmation

I am experiencing a tremendous sense of fulfillment and joy as I turn life's lemons into lemonade.

Mend Your Fences 26

...before someone you care about gets hurt!

A young man was awakened from a deep sleep early one morning by a telephone call. On the other end of the line was an anonymous caller who asked, "Have you looked outside this morning? Your cattle are out on the road headed for the highway." The young man, who was the caretaker of a large ranch, jumped up and ran outside to see almost a hundred head of cattle meandering down the road, headed for the highway about a quarter-mile away.

He ran to the barn, grabbed a bucket of feed, and took off in pursuit of the herd. A bull was in the lead, and by this time, about 50 yards away from the highway. The young man stuck the bucket of feed up to the nose of the bull and enticed him to turn around. As he led the bull back down the road, each cow turned and followed in single file. He felt like the Pied Piper of cattle as he led them all back into the pasture.

After securing the herd of cattle he found a small break in the fence, which he quickly mended to keep them from escaping again. The break was quite small and it surprised him that such large beasts were able to slip through.

Later, the young man reflected on what had happened and pondered the message that life had to teach him from this incident. He thought about the metaphor of fence-mending in his own life—how at times, small, seemingly harmless rifts with family and friends had allowed all kinds of beasts to slip out and cause havoc in his life and the lives of those he loved.

We all have occasional fence-mending to do. That's all part of building community. Words are spoken without thinking, meanings are misunderstood, feelings get hurt, and fences get broken. It's up to us to mend those fences before the beasts get out and someone gets seriously hurt. **Have you had your wake-up call?**

Application

Is there some fence-mending that needs to take place in your life? Is there someone that you have been avoiding because of a longstanding disagreement or misunderstanding? If you don't make an effort to do some fence-mending, there is a risk that others may get hurt, too. Even the smallest break can set a herd of beasts on the loose. So, grab your tools and go mend your fence.

Perhaps the most effective fence-mending tool you have is the words, "I'm sorry." It's practically impossible for someone to fight with you when you are willing to negotiate surrender. It doesn't matter who started the rift or how long it's been going on. It is in **your** best interest to resolve it. Surrender does not mean that you are a weak milquetoast or doormat for others to walk over. Surrender is about detaching from your or anyone else's need to be right. By doing so, you will be at peace with everyone in your life, including yourself, and free to enjoy success and abundance.

Affirmation

I am at peace with everyone in my life and completely free to enjoy success and abundance.

Name It, Then Claim It

27

Be specific about what you want!

A cartoon appeared recently in a local newspaper that depicted two men, manacled in chains, rowing in the galley of a slave ship. One says to the other, "I always wanted to be somebody, but I should have been more specific." Phillip McGraw, author of *Life Strategies*, says that the act of naming and claiming what you want is one of the top ten Life Laws that govern our world. He says, "Not knowing precisely what you want is not okay. If you cannot name, and name with great specificity, what it is that you want, then you will never be able to step up and claim it."

Yogi Berra once said, "If you don't know where you're going, you might end up some place else." Unless you are very specific about what you want in life, you may end up with a lot of things you don't want. That's an all-too-familiar situation for many of us. From past experience, we can speak with great confidence about the things we don't want. Therein lies a danger: because of the law of attraction, the more we focus on what we don't want, the more of it we get. And you can never get enough of what you don't want!

Successful people are very deliberate about the pursuit of their life goals. They know specifically what they want, then fix their sights and take aim with careful precision. Decisiveness creates action, and action leads to results.

Don't be shy about the fact that you want extraordinary things in life. You deserve them! Acknowledge and honor the special feelings of self-worth, significance, and fulfillment you gain from receiving those things. Be ambitious, yet realistic with your goals. Aim for a realistic target that you can hit, but don't set your sights too low and spend your life working for things you don't want. **What you want is yours for the asking. Be specific!**

Application

Ask yourself the following questions:

⚜ What do I really want in life?

⚜ Why do I want it?

⚜ What am I willing to do to get it?

⚜ Who do I need to enlist to help me get it?

⚜ How will I feel when I get it?

Repeat the process, either alone or with a partner. Be honest with yourself, be sincere, and above all, be specific. The more you practice this, the more you will understand and grasp what it is that you really want in your life. Write some positive affirmations around each of those five areas and expect great things to happen.

Affirmation

I experience abundance in my life by specifically naming and claiming what I really want.

Never Give Up

28

The harvest is waiting!

*I*n the twilight of his career, Winston Churchill was asked to give a speech at the English prep school that he had attended as a boy. The headmaster of the school assured the boys that this would be an historic moment in their lives. He lauded Sir Winston as one of the great orators of the English language and urged the boys to write down every word he said, because his speech was sure to be unforgettable.

When Churchill walked to the podium to deliver his speech, he gazed out over the top of his glasses and spoke the following words: "Never! never! never! never! give up!" Having said that, he walked back to his chair and sat down. His speech was completed.

Though many of the students were disappointed by the abruptness of his speech, the headmaster knew that it may well have been one of his greatest, because it captured the essence of Churchill's character. His "never give up" attitude inspired an entire country to continue to fight under the bleakest of circumstances, when others might have surrendered. Consequently, a great victory was won and the people of England experienced successful living, in large part because of Winston Churchill's relentless leadership.

St. Paul said, "Let us not become weary in doing good, for at the proper time we will reap a harvest if we do not give up" (Galatians 6:9). The harvest awaits you. In due time, your commitment to stay the course will reap generous rewards. As Thoreau taught, "If one advances confidently in the direction of his dreams, and endeavors to live the life which he has imagined, he will meet with a success unexpected in common hours." **Good things come to those who never give up!**

Application

Do you have a tendency to give up when the projects of life become mundane, tedious, or difficult? Does success seem to continually elude you or stand just beyond your grasp? A few people seem to be born with the strength to overcome any obstacle in their lives, but the majority of us have to work on developing our "stick-to-itiveness" muscles. Just as an athlete trains for competition by the gradual strengthening of her body, you can increase your mental and emotional stamina by training yourself to finish the races in your life.

Start with small projects that you can finish in a day or two. Experience the taste of personal accomplishment and increase your levels of confidence by completing small goals. Success breeds success. As your confidence grows, you will find that you will possess a greater capacity to pursue larger endeavors and challenges. Use daily visualization and affirmations to create a picture of what you want to accomplish in your mind. Commit each day to move one step closer to your dream, and follow Churchill's advice: "Never! never! never! never! give up!"

Affirmation

I experience success in my life by persistently moving towards my dreams each day.

Open Your Heart 29

...and let the walls come down!

*O*ne of the more interesting Old Testament stories is the account of
Joshua and the battle of Jericho. In this widely told story, Joshua,
Moses' heir apparent, led the army of Israel in a rather peculiar battle plan
to bring down the walls of the city of Jericho. For six days, all the soldiers
in Joshua's army and seven priests carrying the Ark of the Covenant
marched once a day around the walls of Jericho. On the seventh day, they
marched around Jericho seven times, then blew their trumpets. At the
sound of the trumpets on the seventh day, the walls of Jericho came tum-
bling down and Joshua's army won a great battle.

At that time, Jericho was a small, yet strategic city for that geographi-
cal area. It was at the heart of many trade routes, offering much economic
and social stability for those who controlled it. Joshua's army displayed
great courage, and faith in divine power, by marching around the city for
seven days to bring down the walls that stood between them and victory.

This story provides a lesson of major symbolic significance for us. Most
of us have a Jericho residing within us. Throughout our lives we have built
walls around our hearts, constructed of fear, mistrust, anger, and other
emotions, which serve to stabilize and isolate us from the rest of the
world. We must bring those walls down to truly experience the freedom
to live successfully. And the only way we can achieve that is through our
collaboration with divine power.

Miracles in our lives require two things from us: a particle of belief, and
a willingness to act upon that belief. Jesus said, "If you have faith as a
grain of mustard seed, you will say to this mountain, 'Move from here to
there,' and it will move; and nothing will be impossible to you."

Open your heart today. Begin your path to freedom by visualizing
yourself marching around the walls that hold you captive. Believe that it

is the Infinite One who causes the walls to tumble as you **blow your trumpet of victory!**

Application

How open is your heart? Are you willing to risk the vulnerability of tearing down the walls that have kept you isolated from others? Perhaps you have been hurt in the past by those you have allowed inside. You may feel that you have been treated unfairly, and you may be right. It's true that building some walls may offer temporary emotional stability, but closing your heart will ultimately cheat you out of the opportunity to fully experience the joy of meaningful relationships.

Be honest with yourself. Resolve now that you will no longer use excuses, rationalizations, and justifications to keep others at arm's length. Begin by finding one other person with whom you can be real. If you can't find that person, ask for divine help to send one your way. And when that one comes, let the walls come down and disclose your true self to him or her. Gather the courage to take off the mask and allow them to see who you really are, warts and all. This process will soon become a template for tearing down the walls with others and building excellent personal relationships, as well as powerful professional alliances.

Affirmation

I open my heart to experience the joy and happiness of meaningful relationships.

Own Your Actions 30

The buck stops with you!

A certain king, who lived a few thousand years ago, fell in love with a beautiful young woman. There was one glaring problem with this relationship: the woman was married. Not only was she a married woman, her husband was one of the most loyal officers in the king's army. The plot thickened when the young woman turned up pregnant with the king's child, and in his desperation to have her for himself, the king finagled a plan to put her husband on the front lines of battle to face sure death.

The king's oldest and wisest advisor got wind of the whole sordid affair and confronted the king with this story: There was a rich man with many flocks, and a poor man who had nothing but one little ewe lamb, which he had bought, nurtured, and loved. One day the rich man stole the little ewe lamb from the poor man and had it served up in a feast for one of his houseguests. This story incensed the king, who angrily declared, "The man who has done this deserves to die, because he had no pity."

The old advisor coldly responded, "Sire, you are that man!" The grief-stricken king gazed sadly into the old sage's eyes and replied, "I, alone, have sinned against God."

This was a king of large proportions, both materially and spiritually. He was the wealthiest man in his world, and was also referred to as "a man after God's own heart." His position was so powerful that he could have rebuffed the old prophet and had his head removed, but instead he chose to humbly acknowledge and assume personal responsibility for his actions. The king still faced consequences for his current actions, but he didn't weave more tangled webs for the future by choosing a course of denial or passing the blame.

We learn from this story that regardless of what measures we take to conceal secrets in our lives, our actions always reveal them to the world.

"Who we are speaks louder than what we say." If no one else will, our actions will eventually hold us accountable. And reproof may come from the humblest of origins, sometimes an old person or a child. When it inevitably comes, the wisest choice is to **take ownership of your action.**

Application

Taking ownership of your actions is one of the most important keys for opening the door to successful living. It entails becoming accountable to someone or something. Many great people, like the king in the story above, have fallen because they became disconnected from their Source of accountability. Fortunately, you can learn from others' actions. Set up an accountability net for yourself. Choose one or two good friends to confidentially share the details of your life with and invite them to give totally honest feedback. Be willing to humbly listen to reproof of your actions without nursing, cursing, or rehearsing the offenses that have occurred. Keep a teachable spirit.

If you want to change your actions, change your thoughts. Think, see, and feel the actions that you want to create. Nothing is real, unless you make it.

Affirmation

I am accountable for my thoughts and actions to those who lovingly reveal direction for my highest good.

Prayer

31

...your connection to the Power Source!

*I*n *The Song of the Bird,* Anthony de Mello tells the story of a bishop whose ship stopped at a remote island for a day. Determined to use the time as profitably as possible, he strolled along the seashore and came across three fishermen mending their nets. In pidgin English they explained to him that centuries before they had been Christianized by missionaries. "We Christians!" they said, proudly pointing to one another. The bishop was impressed. Did they know the Lord's Prayer? They had never heard of it. This bishop was shocked.

"What do you say, then, when you pray?" he asked. They responded, "We lift eyes to heaven. We pray, "We are three, you are three, have mercy on us." The bishop was appalled at the primitive, downright heretical nature of their prayer. So he spent the whole day teaching them the Lord's Prayer. The fishermen were poor learners, but they gave it all they had, and before the bishop sailed away the next day he had the satisfaction of hearing them go through the whole formula without a fault.

Months later, the bishop's ship happened to pass by those islands again, and the bishop, as he paced the deck saying his evening prayers, recalled with pleasure the three men on that distant island who were now able to pray, thanks to his patient efforts. While he was lost in that thought, he happened to look up and noticed a spot of light in the east. The light kept approaching the ship, and as the bishop gazed in wonder, he saw three figures *walking on the water.* The captain stopped the ship, and everyone leaned over the rails to see this sight.

When they were within speaking distance, the bishop recognized his three friends, the fishermen. "Bishop!" they exclaimed. "We hear your boat go past island and come hurry hurry meet you."

"What is it you want?" asked the awe-stricken bishop. "Bishop," they said, "we so, so sorry. We forget lovely prayer. We say, 'Our Father in heaven, holy be your name, your kingdom come . . .' then we forget. Please tell us prayer again."

The bishop felt humbled. "Go back to your homes, my friends," he said, "and each time you pray say, 'We are three, you are three, have mercy on us!'"

A common thread in the fabric of successful people is belief in a Divine Source and a regular practice of some form of prayer. Prayer has power, not through religious verbiage or eloquent speech, but through simple, childlike belief and acceptance. **Prayer is not about changing God, it is about changing us!**

Application

The most effective prayer is to recognize God as the Infinite Source of all supply, and affirm that you are connected to that Infinite Source. Through that realization, simply align yourself with the mind of God by agreeing that you have everything you need in the present moment to experience peace and unlimited abundance. Then with gratitude, let go and let God.

Affirmation

I gratefully affirm that God is the source of all abundance in my life.

Prepare for Opportunity **32**

...and play for the love of the game!

*I*n his prime, Larry Bird of the Boston Celtics was one of the most complete basketball players of all time. Although he wasn't able to run as fast or jump as high as many of the players in the National Basketball Association, he was named Rookie of the Year in 1980, Most Valuable Player in two championship series, and league MVP for three consecutive years. After leading the Celtics to the NBA Championship in 1986, Bird was asked what he planned to do next. "I've still got some things I want to work on," he replied. "I'll start my off-season training next week. Two hours a day, with at least a hundred free throws."

Larry Bird was known to be relentless in his commitment to practice. He would usually show up on the court an hour or two before his teammates got to practice to work on his shots—free throws, fade-away jumpers, and three-pointers from all angles. When faced with game situations, his preparation enabled him to capitalize on every opportunity with graceful precision.

No doubt, Larry Bird loved to win. Still, his desire for championship rings was not the driving force that motivated him to practice so diligently and play so wholeheartedly. According to his agent, "He did it to enjoy himself. Not to make money, to get acclaim, to get stature. He just loves to play basketball."

We're all faced with opportunities for greatness. We may not be called upon to help win an NBA championship, but each of us has the chance to contribute MVP performances for teams of which we are members. Those teams may be our family, our work partnerships, or our church or civic communities.

The key to our own success, like Larry Bird's, rides on our willingness to Practice! Practice! Practice! . . . and a burning desire to seize each moment of opportunity because of our love for the game. **Success is where preparation and passion meet opportunity.**

Application

Opportunity knocks, are you listening? Abraham Lincoln once said, "If I had ten hours to cut trees, I would spend eight hours sharpening my saw." How are you preparing for those inevitable opportunities that are coming your way? Commit to set aside time each day for sharpening your own saw. Decide what you really have a passion for in life and begin to develop the skills that are required to do it. You may need to enroll in classes at your local college, university, or vocational-tech school. Many schools have excellent correspondence or Internet-based courses available, which will allow you to study at home. Check your newspaper for groups that meet in your community to share common interests. Through the Universal Law of Attraction, what you invest your time and passion in will be drawn back to you with magnetic force, and the doors of opportunity will open wide.

Affirmation

I create and attract opportunities into my life through investments of time and passion.

Quality of Life   *33*

Choose the most important things first!

*T*he professor set a glass jar on the table in front of the classroom, then took some large rocks out of a bag and placed them inside the jar. When the rocks were stacked up to the top rim of the jar, he asked his students if they thought the jar was full. The students nodded in agreement. He then pulled out a bag of small pebbles and began pouring them into the jar, filling the crevices and gaps between the large rocks. He asked again if the students thought the jar was full. They began to suspect that the professor had something else up his sleeve, so most of them shook their heads no. As they suspected, he pulled out yet another bag with finely granulated sand in it. He poured the sand into the jar, filling up the smaller gaps between the rocks and pebbles. He asked the students once again if they thought it was full. Some nodded and others shook their heads, suspicious that something else was coming. The professor then pulled out a glass of water and filled the jar until it was overflowing. At that point everyone in the class agreed that the jar was finally full.

"So what's the point?" asked the professor. Many of the students interpreted the message to be, "There's always room for more." He concurred that was a good observation, but not the point he was trying to make. He told them that if he had not placed the big rocks into the jar first, there would not have been room for all of them. He said, "The big rocks represent the most important people and things in your life. If you don't fit them in first, there won't be room for them when your life gets filled with the little stuff."

Life has a surface and a depth. The depth contains the big rocks, the things that have the greatest importance and lasting value for us. When we acknowledge those and choose to make them our top priority, our quality of life improves. **Make your life successful by choosing first things first!**

Application

What are the big rocks in your life? Are you putting them in the jar first? Decide who and what are most important to you and commit to making sure they fit into your life first. You may need to take an inventory of your life to decide your priorities. Write on a piece of paper the heading, "What Really Matters in My Life," and list below all the people and things you consider to be important in your life. Then go back and number those in their order of importance to you. Start with number one as the most important and work down. When the small rocks show up, wanting a space in the jar of your life, check first to see if the most important ones have been taken care of. Get used to the idea that "No." is a complete sentence. You can say no without offering excuses or apologies. And every "no" you give to the small rocks frees up more space to say "yes" to the bigger, more important ones.

Affirmation

I live a quality-filled life by choosing the most important people and things in my life first.

Quiet Solitude 34

Discover a peace beyond human understanding!

*A*n old Zen story recounts how once upon a time there was a bed of squashes ripening in the corner of a field. One day they began quarrelling. The squashes split up into factions and made a lot of noise shouting at one another. The head priest of a nearby temple, hearing the sound, rushed out to see what was wrong. He scolded the wrangling squashes, saying, "Whatever are you doing? Fighting among yourselves is useless." The priest taught them all how to sit in quiet solitude, and gradually their anger died away. Then the priest said, "Put your hands on top of your heads." The squashes did so and discovered a peculiar thing. Each one had a stem growing from its head, which connected them all one to another and back to a common root. "What a mistake we have made!" the squashes said. "We are all joined to one another, based on the same root and living one life only. In spite of that we quarrel. How foolish our ignorance has been."

According to seventeenth-century French philosopher and scientist, Blaise Pascal, "All man's miseries derive from not being able to sit quietly in a room alone." The daily practice of sitting in quiet solitude produces a calmness of mind and a gentle strength that will help you to remain poised and peaceful. The more you engage in this practice, the greater your success will be and the greater influence and power you will possess.

James Allen, author of *As a Man Thinketh,* said, "The strong, calm man is always loved and revered. He is like a shade-giving tree in a thirsty land, or a sheltering rock in a storm. Who does not love a tranquil heart, a sweet-tempered, balanced life? That exquisite poise of character, which we call serenity, is the last lesson of culture; it is the flowering of life, the fruitage of the soul. **It is precious as wisdom, more desired than gold.**"

Application

Begin the daily practice of sitting in quiet solitude. Sit comfortably alone each morning for ten to fifteen minutes. Close your eyes and begin taking slow, deep breaths. Be aware of your chest as an empty space where your feelings enter. Let your attention rest there, breathe gently, and feel your breath going into the middle of your chest area. Allow your breath to slowly go in and out, and as it does, allow yourself to experience your feelings and thoughts. For the next few minutes just sit and listen. As memories, fears, dreams, and wishes begin to surface in your mind, you might find yourself becoming distracted. Don't try to push them out, just allow those thoughts to flow away and let the experience be what it will be. If your thoughts drift, don't become discouraged; just patiently bring your attention back to your chest area. The more you practice this, the more connected you will begin to feel, with a sense of calmness and inner peace.

Affirmation

I create a sense of calmness, peace, and tranquility by sitting in quiet solitude each day.

Recovery from Stress

35

Making waves for success!

*T*he young woman dashes out of the house in a hurry to get to work. She has already had a full morning of activities getting children ready for school and tending to the needs of her family. She has a very important meeting this morning and she knows that her boss is depending on her to be there, on time. As she turns onto the on-ramp for the freeway, the woman's heart sinks. There is bumper-to-bumper traffic as cars in front of her are moving at fifteen miles per hour in a sixty-five-mile-per-hour zone. She glances at her watch, knowing that she will be late for the important meeting if she continues at this rate. The pressure builds. Her pulse begins to race, her forehead perspires, her hands sweat, and butterflies are flittering furiously in her stomach as she grips the wheel tighter in an attempt to release some of the super-energy that's running through her veins. She experiences another day in the life of a working mother.

Does this scenario sound familiar? Sure it does. Stress is inevitable. We all experience moments of high anxiety and personal pressure on an almost daily basis. The objective of a successful stress management program is not to completely eliminate stress from our lives, but to ensure that we have adequate moments of recovery.

Stress can be a beneficial force in our lives if we choose to harness its energy in a positive way. World-class athletes constantly utilize stress, induced through intensive training, to strengthen them. They create intervals of stress, followed by longer periods of recovery, to push themselves to greater levels of physical conditioning and personal achievement. You can do the same as you **learn to rest for success!**

Application

Developing a stress recovery program in your life will require acts of self-care on your part. If you were arrested for being good to yourself, hopefully there would be enough evidence to convict you. Use the following suggestions to build your foundation of self-care and stress management:

※ **Sleep.** This is the #1 recovery factor for stress. Adequate amounts of sleep for the average person should be six to eight hours per night.

※ **Diet.** Eat light, eat often, and eat a variety of foods. For peak performance, eat higher amounts of protein during the morning and afternoon, and more complex carbohydrates, such as pastas and vegetables, during the evening.

※ **Exercise.** Make it fun and painless. An adequate exercise program should include daily aerobic activities, such as walking, jogging, biking, or swimming, and light weight-lifting exercises several times a week for strengthening bones and muscles.

※ **Humor.** Learn to laugh at yourself and don't sweat the small stuff!

Affirmation

I allow stress to strengthen and energize me as I practice healthy recovery techniques each day.

Relationships

36

Partnering for peak performance!

*B*ooker T. Washington was the foremost black educator of the late nineteenth and early twentieth centuries. Born a slave on a small farm in the Virginia backcountry, he rose to prominence in 1881 when he founded the Tuskegee Institute in the Black Belt of Alabama. A story is told about an incident that happened to Dr. Washington on his way to his office at Tuskegee one wintry morning. As he was walking past a large estate, the woman who owned the place walked out of the house and, mistaking him for one of the hired servants, shouted orders for him to chop some firewood and bring it inside.

Rather than becoming indignant, Dr. Washington took off his coat and began to chop wood. When he finished, he carried the wood into the house and stacked it, then continued on his way to work. One of the girls who worked in the kitchen recognized him and told the owner who he was. The owner was quite embarrassed by her presumptuousness and hastily went to find him at Tuskegee to offer her apologies.

When she found Dr. Washington at his office she apologized profusely and let him know how embarrassed she was about the whole incident. He responded, "That's no problem, ma'am. I love to work and I love to help my friends." The woman, who was quite wealthy, was so touched by his gracious spirit that she reportedly became a generous financial contributor and ardent vocal supporter of Dr. Washington and the Tuskegee Institute throughout the rest of her life.

Like Booker T. Washington, think of the entire world as your friend, and be a friend to the world in return. Refuse to see the negative side of anyone. Your love and understanding of others is reflected back to you. As you help, you are helped. As you uplift, you are uplifted. As you think and act in ways that are loving and harmonious, you will transform your life and **find friendship, love, appreciation, and support.**

Application

Your success can be catapulted to new heights through establishing collaborative relationships with others. One of the best ways to get what you want in life is to help someone else get what they want. Your personal relationships are the fertile soil from which your advancement, success, and achievement in life will grow. You cannot hold a torch to light another's path without brightening your own.

Affirmation

I am supportive and loving toward everyone and desire each person's good as I desire my own.

Self-Confidence 37

Learn the art of playing large!

*T*he teacher asked her first graders to draw a picture of a personal hero or someone they admired. As she walked around the room, one particular drawing caught her eye. She approached the young boy who drew it and said, "That's a very nice picture, Johnny. Who is it?" Little Johnny radiantly proclaimed, "It's God!" "But no one knows what God looks like," the teacher said. "They will when I get finished!" he confidently replied.

Children are among the greatest models of self-confidence. Without any sentimentality, Jesus said, "Whoever among you becomes as a child shall know the Kingdom!"

In his 1994 inaugural speech, Nelson Mandela expressed the thought, "We ask ourselves, 'Who am I to be brilliant, gorgeous, talented and fabulous?' Actually, who are you not to be? You are a child of God!" Your playing large serves the world much better than playing small. Rest in the confidence that you are the light of God individualized.

As you allow your own light to shine, you'll give others permission to do the same. It has been said that when Jesus, Buddha, Gandhi, or Mother Teresa entered a village, the consciousness of the entire community was raised. The more liberated you become to confidently experience your own greatness, the more **your presence liberates others.**

Application

Self-confidence is your most important asset for successful living. It is both a clear understanding of what you can do and a clear vision of what you can become. Self-confidence is the basis for personal belief in yourself, in what you do, and in the ideas and dreams you have.

There are several ways to improve your self-confidence. First, strengthen your belief system through the use of daily positive affirmations. Repeat these affirmations several times a day to yourself, allowing them to be fully embraced by your subconscious, which will in turn bring those beliefs into the world of physical form.

Act as if you are confident in what you are doing. As you exude self-confidence, others will perceive it and mirror it back to you. Set goals to accomplish something quickly attainable and follow through with them. Success breeds success. The path to self-confidence is in doing the things you fear. And as you record successful experiences behind you, your achievements will grow, and so will your self-confidence.

Affirmation

I am confidently and successfully living to my highest ability, knowing that I am the Light of God individualized.

Seize the Day 38

Live in the Present!

*J*ohn Bunyan, the seventeenth-century preacher and author of *Pilgrim's Progress*, once said that he was able to eliminate worry from two days of each week. He wrote: "There are two days in the week about which and upon which I never worry. Two carefree days, kept sacredly free from fear and apprehension. One of these days is yesterday and the other is tomorrow."

Siddhartha Gautama, the one called Buddha, said, "Do not pursue the past. Do not lose yourself in the future. The past no longer is, and the future has not yet come. Look deeply at life, just as it is arising in the very here and now. Recognize it—invincible, unshakable. Care for it with your heart and mind."

You were created to carry the weight of twenty-four hours—no more. Now is the only time you can truly feel alive. Dwelling on the past or the future will only diminish your ability to experience joy in the present.

Each day, opportunities come our way and we must decide whether to take a chance or play it safe. Successful people realize that nothing is gained without the willingness to take some risks. It is that *carpe diem*—"seize the day"—spirit that beckons each of us to fully experience a life free of regrets and worry. May that spirit dwell in your heart always, as you live by the words of this Sanskrit proverb, **"Look well to this one day, for it, and it alone, is life."**

Application

Determine to keep your focus on the present. You may have regrets from the past. We all do, but instead of saying, "If only . . . ," when those thoughts of the past come up, say, "Next time . . ."

With the dawning of each new day, commit to do your best, no more and no less. Also, keep in mind that your best may change from moment to moment. Don't beat yourself up when you fall down. Simply get up, determined to do your best next time. You are here to experience joy, happiness, and love in the present moment.

Do not agonize over the future. Jesus said, "Who of you by worrying can add a single hour to his life?" Fretting over the future will drain your life energy. You don't need to prove anything to anyone. Just be yourself, play it loose, and enjoy life. Say no when you want to say no, and yes when you want to say yes. You have the inalienable right to be who you are. Remember these words from David Whyte's *The House of Belonging:* "Anything or anyone that does not bring you alive is too small for you."

Affirmation

I am free to live in the present in a wonderful state of inner peace and passion for life.

Thoughts 39

Cultivate the garden of your mind!

James Allen (1864–1912) was a master horticulturist who was devoted to the timeless art of cultivating the garden of the mind. Throughout his life he wrote a series of powerful treatises on the creative power of positive thinking. In his most famous work, *As a Man Thinketh*, Allen wrote, "Act is the blossom of thought, and joy and suffering are its fruits; thus does a man garner in the sweet and bitter fruitage of his own husbandry."

Our mind may be compared to a garden, which may be thoughtfully and deliberately cultivated or allowed to run wild. Whether cultivated or neglected, the garden of the mind is certain to bring forth fruit. Creation is the natural order of life. We cannot *not* create! As Allen said, "If no useful seeds are put into it [the mind], then an abundance of useless weed seeds will fall therein, and will continue to produce their kind."

Every seed of thought that is sown, or allowed to take root in the mind, will blossom sooner or later into its own kind. The internal world of thought manifests itself into the external world of circumstance. If we think of failure, failure will be ours. If we think of success, success will be ours. For what we think will come about. Napoleon Hill said, "Whatever the mind of man can conceive and believe, it can achieve."

In the light of this truth, rather than continually struggling to initiate changes at the *effect* level in your life, it makes much more sense to facilitate changes at the *cause* level: your thoughts. Cultivate the garden of your mind by visualizing good health, happiness, successful relationships, and other desires for your life. Imagine getting exactly what you want in life. The more passionate you feel about what you visualize, the greater the energy you'll summon to create it. **Change your mind, and you'll change your life!**

Application

Lao-tzu once said, "He who knows how to plant, shall not have his plant uprooted; he who knows how to hold a thing, shall not have it taken away." Firmly cultivate the garden of your mind by setting aside some time each day for the purpose of planting and watering the seeds of your desires. As great artisans and skilled craftsmen become accomplished through much practice, so will you become a master at creating what you want by the daily practice of tending to your mental garden. One of the most effective ways to do this is to write down your thoughts, or make a dream board by cutting and pasting pictures to a poster board to create a visual representation of your desires. Review your written list or dream board once or twice each day. Repeat positive affirmations out loud to yourself when you first get up in the morning and before you go to bed at night. Visualize yourself in those pictures in your dream board and act as if everything there is already present in your life. Your thoughts will create the reality you want!

Affirmation

As the master gardener of my mind, I successfully create a life that is blossoming with happiness, joy, and love.

Trust the Process 40

The process is part of the gift!

*I*n *Building Your Field of Dreams,* Mary Manin Morrissey tells the story of a teacher in Africa with the Peace Corps who received a beautiful seashell from a man whom she had been assisting. Knowing that the ocean was some thirty miles away from where the man lived, and that there were no cars or means of motorized transportation in his remote village, she was a little confused. "Where did you find this?" she asked him. "Did a trader bring it to your village?"

"No, no," the man said, and then he told her that he had walked to a town on the coast.

She said, "You walked thirty miles to bring me a seashell? That is sixty miles round trip! Thank you!"

"Yes," the man acknowledged. "Long walk part of gift."

The process of dream-building is a long, sometimes arduous, walk for most of us. But we must learn to trust the process, for it is ultimately part of the gift. When we speak of trust, we tend to equate it with faith, or belief. But the word "trust" has a slightly different meaning from "faith," which usually requires an object, as in "faith in __." Trust is more of an attitude than a belief. It is the acceptance of the infinite abundance of the present.

Such was the attitude that Jesus espoused when he implored his students to imitate the sparrows and the lilies of the field. They never labor, nor worry, about tomorrow. Trusting the process is a commitment to **open your heart and mind to all the creative possibilities of the moment.**

Application

Perhaps you have become discouraged on your own journey towards your dreams. The walk has been longer than you expected, you're tired, afraid, and may have even taken a wrong turn or two. Don't give up. Trust the process. Each step you take will produce benefits beyond what you have imagined. Ultimately the walk is worth it. It is part of the gift. If you continue to press onward in the direction of your dream, you will reap a far greater reward than the home, the work, or the relationship that was the original object of your desire. You will experience a grander vision as you discover that, instead of you building your dream, your dream has been building you.

Affirmation

I joyfully trust the process and accept the infinite abundance of the present moment.

Unity Consciousness 41

Think globally, act locally!

*I*n the 1940s and 1950s a frightening disease called poliomyelitis ran rampant throughout the country. The polio virus was feared especially because it made children very ill, leaving them disabled or paralyzed for life. Parents, who were terrified that their children would contract this dreaded disease, pleaded for someone in the world of medicine and science to do something to help.

Jonas Edward Salk heard that plea. Born in New York City in 1914, Salk was a microbiologist who went to work on finding a vaccine to prevent the spread of the disease. He took samples of the virus, killed them and sterilized them, and gave them to people as shots. When Salk injected the dead virus into people, their bodies built up antibodies for the polio germ. Afterwards, when people were infected with the live virus, their bodies were able to win the fight against it without getting sick. This was a phenomenal discovery and a dream come true for parents and children all over the world. In 1953, Salk introduced his vaccine to the world, and one of the most frightening and dangerous diseases of history is now almost completely extinct.

Dr. Salk planned and developed an institute for biological studies, bringing together scientists and scholars from many fields of research who shared a common interest in science and a concern for the implications of their work, both for the individual and for society as a whole. Today, the internationally prestigious Salk Institute for Biological Studies is a beacon of hope for millions.

His scientific and medical endeavors changed the lives of millions of people, but Jonas Salk's greatest passion was working on the cure for war—in his words, "finding a cure for the cancer of the world." He devoted most of his boundless energy to traveling to international conferences and speaking to world leaders about the importance of peace. He has been honored with dozens of awards, including the Presidential Medal of Freedom and the Nehru Award for International Understanding. Dr. Salk gave the world hope for freedom from polio. But more importantly, he helped to give the world hope for **the freedom to live in peace.**

Application

How can you contribute to peace in your world? The first step is gaining an awareness that it is essential that we all act together, as human beings, to support our common needs for survival and fulfillment. We share a global destiny that transcends all our differences, such as race, sex, religion, class, culture, and nationality. By simply affirming our common humanness and bringing it to the foreground of our thoughts, we are more likely to act together with other humans to meet our communal needs and shared aspirations.

The step after awareness is choosing a deliberate course of action. Nothing happens quite by chance. Success is spawned by the accumulation of information and experience. Commit to becoming active, by volunteering your time and financial support to causes that benefit the physical, mental, emotional, and spiritual well-being of the members of your community, and ultimately the world.

Affirmation

I contribute to world peace and harmony through unity consciousness.

Use Life's Levers

42

... to strengthen your position!

Y ou have a massive stone to lift into place and plenty of people to help you, but all you get is a bunch of people grunting. What do you do? Turn to a lever, of course. A lever is a type of simple machine that makes lifting heavy objects easier. The lever sits on a fulcrum. This is the pivot point that allows the lever to tilt to the heavier side when there is uneven weight. The load is the amount of weight that is put on one side, and this amount makes the lever tilt to the heavier side. The effort is the amount of weight added to the other side of the lever, which allows it to balance. Balance means that the weights on each side of the lever equal out, and the lever becomes straight.

Try your hand at investigating how levers work with the following activity:

1 Set up a lever by placing a ruler on top of a pencil. The ruler acts as the two lever arms. The pencil that it pivots or balances on is called the fulcrum.
2 Place a load of five coins or washers (taped together in a stack) at one end of the ruler on the 2.5 cm (1 in.) mark.
3 Lift the load by pressing down at the opposite end of the ruler using one finger. Notice how hard you need to press to lift the load.
4 Change the position of the pencil and press to lift the load. Try several different positions. Each time notice how hard you press in order to lift the load.

In the activity above you observed that the closer you moved the fulcrum to the load, the easier it became to lift. Now think of how you might apply the various emotional and mental levers in your life to gain the leverage you need to accomplish your goals and dreams. Emotions, such as feelings of love, anger, and fear, create a tremendous amount of energy that can be harnessed as a lever to strengthen you. **Use every situation and emotion you experience to lift you to success!**

Application

What are the levers in your life? What is your burning passion? What conjures up an all-consuming feeling of love for you? Are you angry with someone or something? Perhaps you have an overwhelming fear or phobia. Every one of these emotions will help to produce energy that can be utilized for leverage to strengthen you. As with the fulcrum and the lever, the closer you put the emotion to the load you want to lift, the lighter it will seem. The next time you become angry with someone, ask yourself, "How can I use the energy I feel at this moment to strengthen me for a positive outcome?" The next time you have an overwhelming sense of fear, ask, "What can I do to make this fear serve as a lever in my life?"

The most powerful of all emotional levers is love. Love will supply you with supernatural strength to accomplish the greatest of feats. No situation or emotion in life need be wasted. Use all things to your advantage for successful living.

Affirmation

I am using every situation and emotion in life as a lever to strengthen me.

Validate Those You Appreciate 43

Take a little love and pass it on!

A group of graduate students was given an assignment by one of their professors. She gave each student three buttons that had the words "Who You Are Makes a Difference" on them, then proceeded to tell them how special each of them was and how they had made a difference in her life. The professor told them to "pay it forward" by seeking out and presenting one of the buttons to a person who had made a difference in their life, expressing their own appreciation. The students were instructed to give the third button to this person and ask them to pass it on to someone in their life.

One young man in the class decided he would give a button to the man who ran the company he worked for and express to him what an influence the man had been in his life. The owner of the company was quite touched and a little surprised at the young man's gesture. The young man told his boss about the school project, then gave him the other button and asked him to pass it on to someone that made a difference in his life.

The man thought some time about who might be the recipient of his button, and decided to give it to his sixteen-year-old son. When the man got home from work that evening, he went to his son's room and slipped the button into his hand. He hugged the boy and told him what a difference he had made in his life and how proud he was to be his father.

Upon listening to his father's words, the boy began to weep. He confessed to his father that he felt like a failure and completely unloved. In his despondency the boy had decided to take his own life that very night and put an end to his anguish. Fortunately, this father's well-timed words of validation and encouragement became a lifeline to a young son drowning in hopelessness and despair.

You never know when your words of love and appreciation may save someone else's life. We all need to be validated from time to time. One of our greatest needs as human beings is to feel important to others in our life. And the greatest way to get our own needs met is to give what we need. **Let's Offer Validation and Encouragement (L.O.V.E.) to others, and receive L.O.V.E. in return!**

Application

Get into the habit of validating and encouraging the people in your life. Make some "Who You Are Makes a Difference" buttons or stickers and pass them out to those who touch you and make a difference in your life. Begin leaving little notes for your spouse, children, work partners, and coworkers. Tell them how much you appreciate them and how important they really are to you. You have the power to make others feel good about themselves ... and you'll feel better about yourself as you do.

Affirmation

I validate the people in my life and pass love on each day, to make the world a better place to live.

Vision

The art of seeing the unseen

A few years ago, a group of journalists was given a tour of the EPCOT Center at Disney World in Orlando, Florida. Their guide explained that Walt Disney had a dream in the early 1960s of building an entire city. This city would be called an Experimental Prototype Community of Tomorrow, or EPCOT for short. It would be a model community that would serve as both an example for optimal living and a laboratory to test solutions to problems that other cities face, such as urban unrest, suburban sprawl, increasing crime, air and water pollution, overtaxed roads, and overtaxed citizens.

Disney bought thousands of acres of land in Florida and persuaded the Florida Legislature to grant his company the power to drain, dredge, and develop the land into his dream city. He threw himself into this "Florida Project," which was to consume his final days. First he planned to build a theme park and resort, which would be used to pay for the rest of the development. Although he had already built Disneyland in California, the world's most successful theme park, the EPCOT Center proved to be his greatest challenge.

Walt Disney died in 1966, his plans far from complete. Roy Disney, Walt's brother, continued to carry on with his work. Magic Kingdom Theme Park and its associated hotels that comprised Walt Disney World opened in October 1971. The EPCOT dream fell by the wayside at that time, but was reborn a decade later. EPCOT Center opened on October 1, 1982, over twenty years after Walt Disney had conceived his dream.

After the tour guide told this story to the visiting journalists, one young writer gazed up at EPCOT Center and observed, "It's too bad the old man didn't live to see it!" The guide quickly responded, "Oh, Mr. Disney saw it all right. If he hadn't, it wouldn't be here today!"

Visionary people have a knack for "seeing the unseen." Viktor Frankl, the renowned Viennese psychiatrist who survived years of torture in a Nazi concentration camp, once spoke these words to an audience: "There's one reason why I'm here today. What kept me alive in a situation where others had given up hope and died was the dream that someday I'd be here telling you how I survived the concentration camps. I've never been here before. I've never seen any of you before. I've never given this speech before. But in my dreams I've stood before you in this room and said these words a thousand times."

Life becomes what we envision it to be!

Application

Are you "seeing the unseen" in your life? Use the creative power of your mind to paint a mental picture of what you want to achieve in life. Don't allow the present circumstances to discourage you, regardless of how bleak they may appear. You have the capability to create what you want in the future. Close your eyes and envision your life as totally successful. See every detail in your mind. Touch it. Smell it. Feel it deeply to the depths of your being. The more vividly you create your vision at the mental and emotional levels, the more powerfully it will be manifested into the physical world. Finally, cast aside all doubt. You'll see it when you believe it!

Affirmation

I experience a wonderfully fulfilling reality through stead-fastly setting my mind upon a grand vision for my life.

Wait

...and good things will come!

*I*f you have ever been to a high school class reunion, you probably discovered that many of the best and brightest students didn't live up to their yearbook predictions of success, while many unpromising classmates found wealth, love, and fame. How can that be?

Daniel Goleman reported in his book, *Emotional Intelligence*, that academic intelligence is not the greatest predictor of lifetime success. Rather, Goleman concludes, emotional intelligence provides a more solid foundation for successful careers, love, marriage, family, and friendships. Perhaps the greatest indicator of emotional intelligence is the ability to delay gratification—to wait.

The Marshmallow Test was devised at Stanford University in the 1960s to measure emotional intelligence. This test was conducted on students in nursery school, whose progress was then charted through the classroom onward into adulthood. In the test, a monitor put one marshmallow down in front of each child with the instruction that, if they waited to eat it until he returned in fifteen minutes, he would reward them with two marshmallows.

As soon as the monitor left the room, one-third of the children grabbed their one marshmallow and ate it. The fifteen minutes the monitor was gone must have seemed like hours to the other children, who were patient enough to wait for the double reward. Some covered their eyes, others put their heads in their arms, while some sang or played games with themselves to pass the time. Years later, the researchers found that those children who had delayed gratification in the Marshmallow Test became adults who were more socially competent, more self-sufficient and assertive, and better able to handle stress and frustration. They also proved to be confident, trustworthy, and responsible.

The ABC's of Successful Living

A world of enjoyment awaits those who can delay gratification. The practice of waiting for gratification does not mean that we must forego pleasure. In fact, restraint actually increases pleasure. In addition to a greater portion of reward, we also receive personal satisfaction for our investment of anticipation. And **waiting provokes gratitude for all of life's gifts!**

Application

This concept may challenge you to rethink your approach to work and some of the other areas of your life. You may have been taught to believe that it is the "movers and shakers" who get ahead in life ... the "early bird gets the worm" philosophy. Fortunately, there's a success path that requires less struggling and striving. Be happy in knowing that there is plenty in the world for everyone. Regardless of your circumstances, there's no need to hurry or become anxious. Learn to wait for the best things in life. There is no place in the entire Universe where abundance is any more present or any less present than where you are right now. So relax, and enjoy the abundance that the Creator is pouring into your lap at this very moment.

Affirmation

I bask in the abundance for which I have peacefully been waiting.

Write Your Own Obituary 46

...and give your life a happy ending!

*I*n the mid 1800s, Alfred Nobel was one of the world's top manufacturers of explosives and other materials used for destruction. He invented dynamite in 1866. The story is told that when his brother Ludwig died, Alfred picked up a copy of the local newspaper to read what it had to say about his brother. He was shocked to discover that a dreadful mistake had been made. The newspaper had confused Alfred with his brother, and to his dismay, the obituary he was reading was his own.

The editors of the newspaper headlined his obituary, "The Master of Destruction Dies." They wrote about Alfred's involvement with the invention of dynamite and elaborated on the powerful force of death and destruction he had brought into the world.

Alfred Nobel was devastated by what he read about himself in the newspaper. He wanted to be known as a man of peace, not destruction. He came to the realization that if his obituary was to be rewritten, he must do it himself by changing the course of his life. Alfred Nobel did just that! His financial contributions led to the creation of the Nobel Foundation, which awards prizes recognizing the world's great contributors in the fields of physics, chemistry, medicine, literature, and economics. Most importantly, because of the Nobel Peace Prize, Alfred Nobel is known throughout the world today as a man who embraced and perpetuated peace, rather than destruction.

Each of us has something to contribute to the world. We can be a force for building up or tearing down. How will your obituary read? What will people say about your life? Like Alfred Nobel, you can write the script for the story of your life. In fact, you're the only person who can. **Choose the legacy that you will leave!**

Application

What would you like to be remembered for? What would you like people to say about you after you're gone? Sit down and write your own obituary. Better yet, write three obituaries about yourself. Write one from the perspective of what your family members have to say about you. Were you loving and kind? Did you validate those in your life who were closest to you? Was your presence in their life uplifting and encouraging? Next write an obituary from the perspective of a friend in your community. Were you helpful to those in need? Did you always have something positive to say when the chips were down for others? Were you involved in causes that promoted peace and harmony in your world? Write one more obituary from the perspective of a coworker. Did you work with integrity? Was your word impeccable? Were you a benevolent leader, or a faithful follower? Learn from this experience as you commit to write a happy ending for your life.

Affirmation

I am living the life I aspire to and leaving a legacy of peace and harmony in the world.

eXpand Your Mental Capacity 47

Engage in the Mastermind process!

*T*he world faced a tremendous challenge rebounding from the Great Depression in the 1930s. The man at the helm of the ship of recovery for America was Franklin D. Roosevelt. And he wisely surrounded himself with the advice, counsel, and collaboration of a group of people who were willing to lend him wholehearted aid in a spirit of unity.

Roosevelt engaged the help of one man, in particular, who was instrumental in organizing a group that helped lead the country back to prosperity. Napoleon Hill, author of the mega-selling book, *Think and Grow Rich,* agreed to work at the White House for the sum of one dollar a year to help the President facilitate the recovery from the Great Depression. At Hill's urging, Roosevelt brought together a group to mastermind a plan for success.

Hill defined a mastermind group as the "coordination of knowledge and effort, in a spirit of harmony between two or more people, for the attainment of a definite purpose." He believed that if "two heads are better than one," an entire team could yield an exponential growth in mental capacity. This form of cooperative alliance, Hill concluded, has been the basis of nearly every great success.

Regardless of what your dream is, being a member of a mastermind group will benefit you. It will create an opportunity to help others achieve their goals, as you draw upon their diverse experiences, knowledge, and contacts to help you achieve your own. Don't underestimate who and what you know. Look for ways to help others and build a reputation as being a giver. You will derive tremendous personal satisfaction from giving and you will advance your own cause as well. Remember the Universal Principle, **"Give and you shall receive!"**

Application

You can use the following steps to develop a powerful mastermind group that will benefit you and others in achieving your dreams and goals.

Step 1: **Select your team members.** The optimal number for a mastermind group is four to eight individuals who will commit to the group for six months to a year. Look for individuals with a blend of skills and experience, who are open and honest about their strengths and needs and willing to contribute freely. New members should be unanimously approved by the group.

Step 2: **Set regularly scheduled meetings.** Optimally the meetings should be held the same day of the week, twice each month. The two-week gap allows members time to implement ideas discussed in the previous meeting and create new ideas for the next meeting. Meetings should last approximately two hours to give everyone in the group adequate time for discussion.

Step 3: **Make agreements.** In the first meeting, establish some group rules for items such as confidentiality, attendance, and punctuality.

Step 4: **Determine your meeting agenda.** Each meeting should include some time to celebrate achievements and to work on goal setting and problem solving. Members should be accountable to one another and come prepared with issues and questions for the group, in addition to offering solutions and suggestions to team members.

Affirmation

I enthusiastically accept the unlimited abundance that comes to me through the mastermind process.

eXpect Change

48

...the only constant!

A young father was watching a football game on television one Sunday afternoon. His eight-year-old son was in the room trying relentlessly to get his daddy to play with him. The newspaper was spread open on the coffee table with a full-page ad showing a picture of the world as seen from a satellite in space, and the man got a great idea for keeping his son occupied. He took a pair of scissors and cut the page up into over a dozen pieces, then gave them to the young boy along with some cellophane tape, saying, "Here, put this picture of the world together with this tape and show Daddy how smart you are." Then he went back to watching his football game.

Within a surprisingly short amount of time, the boy returned with the picture all taped back together in an impressive fashion for a child so young. The father said, "Son, that's really amazing. How did you put that world together so quickly?"

"Daddy, it was easy," the small boy replied. "There was a picture of a man on the other side. So I just put the man together and then the world came together." The father gave his son a big hug and said, "That's right, son, when the man is together, his world comes together, too."

A monumental moment in life arrives when you discover the Truth that things may happen around you, and things may happen to you, but the most important are the things that happen *in* you. When the man is together, his world comes together.

Change is the only constant in life. Seasons come and go, the sun rises and sets, the trees outside your window bear leaves that turn colors and fall, and the years pass, as life flows along like a river current. In doing so, life brings forth new growth. It makes possible the blossoming of joy, harmony, and peace.

A new *you* is constantly being born. Even though you may want to hold on to old ways and former circumstances, deep within your soul you are aware that it is best to let go and simply allow the process of life to unfold. The gift of a successfully abundant life comes when you are willing to release the old and **allow change to work its miracles *within you!***

Application

Change is inevitable. You can flow with it or resist it. The choice is yours. You are where you are in your experience of relationships, job, and financial condition because of what you think. If you want to change your experience, change your thinking. Allow the circumstances of life to till the soil of your divine nature. In doing so, life will bring forth new growth. Be unperturbed by change that is happening around you. Instead, offer gratitude for the renewal and transformation that is constantly taking place in your life.

Affirmation

I rejoice in the process of change and give thanks for the good that it brings.

Yank Your Own Chain

49

...live independently of others' opinions!

A woman sat crying in a counseling session one morning and made the remark, "I know I'm stupid." Her therapist responded, "How do you know you're stupid?" "Because my husband tells me that all the time," the woman answered.

The counselor asked, "And if I told you that you are a Mack truck, would you believe me?" The woman asserted, "Of course not, that would be ridiculous." Her counselor replied, "Why would that be any more ridiculous than you believing you are stupid simply because your husband says so?"

What people say or do is a reflection of who they are. If someone says, "Hey, you're stupid," that is about him, not you. Don't fall into the trap of personalizing what others think or say about you. Highly successful people learn to live independently of others' opinions.

When you make a habit of not personalizing others' opinions, you will avoid the need to constantly defend your own beliefs or actions. And you'll notice that self-doubt and insecurity will give way to self-confidence and personal freedom. Instead of trusting what others say and do, you'll become an autonomous person, trusting your own ability to make responsible choices.

As you become independent of the opinion of others, you will find that you'll be able to open your heart without the worry of being hurt by others. You can say, "I love you," without the fear of being rejected or ridiculed. You can ask for what you need, without appearing weak. You can say yes—with no strings attached—and no—without feeling guilty. You will experience inner peace and happiness as you **choose to follow your own heart!**

Application

Think of all the opinions that are influencing your life today. You may have been carrying some of these opinions around for years. Perhaps someone told you that you were stupid, or fat, or ugly, when you were a child. Are you still being controlled by those opinions? First, acknowledge that the thoughts others imposed upon you were reflections of themselves, and not you. Next, begin to replace your internal dialogue with positive self-talk and affirmations.

Visualize your life as a movie; in that movie you are the director, the producer, and the leading actor. It is your movie. You can write the script and act it out as you wish. Imagine that you are perfect and that you accept and love yourself just the way you are. Each morning when you awaken, start thinking about all the incredible things that you will make happen that day. Think about how fortunate you are to be free from limitations. Get excited about the possibilities that surround you, as you give yourself permission to live independently of the opinions of others.

Affirmation

I am independent of the opinions of others as I follow my own heart down the path of inner peace and happiness.

Yield to Life's Teaching

50

"To be a learner, you've got to be willing to be a fool."

*I*n his book, *Mastery*, George Leonard related a story that happened to him in the late 1960s on a weekend retreat at the Esalen Institute outside of San Francisco. He had happened upon a mountain man, with the long black hair, bold moustache and rough-hewn clothing of a nineteenth-century outlaw, who was apparently giving an informal lesson on playing conga drums. The man was encircled by a group of about eight people. Leonard pulled up to one unoccupied drum and began to join the others, following the instruction as well as he could.

When the session ended, Leonard started to walk away, but the mountain man came after him, grasped his shoulder, and said, "Man, you are a *learner*. I want you to tell me how I can be a learner."

Leonard stood there speechless. This mountain man, an artist and sculptor who lived in the rugged hills of the Los Padres National Wilderness Area along the Big Sur coast of California, wanted Leonard to come to his place, look at his work, and tell him how *he* could be a learner, too.

Somewhat reluctantly, Leonard agreed to make the arduous journey to Los Padres to look at the man's sculptures. When they arrived, the man showed some of his unfinished work and related to Leonard how he had lost his creative spark. He repeated his question again. "Tell me. How can I be a learner?"

Leonard's mind went absolutely blank, as he heard himself saying, "It's simple. To be a learner, you've got to be willing to be a fool."

In order to yield to life's teaching, you must have the courage and the willingness to surrender. In the early stages of any significant new learning, you must surrender your hard-earned proficiency and risk looking like a fool in order to rise to higher levels of proficiency. If you constantly try to stand on your own dignity, you will become rigid and unteachable. Surrender means to keep a "beginner's mind." **There are no experts, only learners.**

Application

Learning practically any new skill will require you to play the fool. At times it will become necessary for you to give up some hard-earned competency in order to rise to the next level. If you're a better-than-average golfer and want to be an excellent golfer, you might well have to give up playing better-than-average golf as you take your game apart and put it back together again. This will be true for almost any skill, especially when you're stuck at a familiar and comfortable level. Don't allow yourself to stay in that "velvet rut." Surrender ... risk being the fool ... and play like nobody's watching!

Affirmation

I am willing to play the fool as I continually learn new skills for successful living.

Zeal

51

Let enthusiasm float your boat!

*T*he story is told of a dispassionate young man who approached the ancient Greek philosopher Socrates and nonchalantly stated, "O great teacher, I come to you for knowledge." Socrates took the young man down to the sea, waded in with him, and then dunked him under the water for thirty seconds. When he let the young man up for air, Socrates asked him to repeat what he wanted.

"Knowledge, O great one," he sputtered. Socrates put him under the water again, that time for a little longer. After repeated dunkings and responses from the young man, Socrates asked, "What do you want?" The young man gasped, "Air! I want air!"

"Good," answered the philosopher. "Now, when you want knowledge as much as you wanted air, you shall have it."

Your enthusiasm will determine your destiny. Your zeal is fuel for your will. If you want anything badly enough, you'll find the willpower to achieve it. All things are possible for the person who is enthusiastic enough.

Don't be surprised if others in our culture view you a little suspiciously as you begin to live with zeal. Sociologist Tony Campolo recently observed, "We are caught up at a particular state in our national ethos in which we're not only materialistic but worse than that; we're becoming emotionally dead as people. We don't sing, we don't dance, we don't even commit sin with much enthusiasm."

In the end, enthusiasm will influence your success more than your personality or intelligence. Make zeal a characteristic of your life and **enthusiastically begin each day with "fire in your belly."**

Application

Give yourself permission to live with zeal. Be enthusiastic about anyone or anything you choose, without fear of criticism. Tell those you love how you feel about them as often as possible. By doing so, you will double the enthusiasm. Think back to when you were just starting your career, or even farther back to when you were a child. What really turned you on? What have you spent hours and hours doing without getting tired of it? Go back and recapture that old enthusiasm. If you've lost that "fire in the belly," find some people who have it and hang out with them for a while. Enthusiasm is contagious. Make it your burning desire to become the most enthusiastic person you know.

Affirmation

I am the most enthusiastic person I know and I share my zeal with everyone I know.

Zone In

52

. . . stay focused on your dream!

A group of young boys devised a plan to fool an old wise man in their village. They plotted to take a small live bird and approach the old man. One of them would hold the bird behind his back and ask, "Is this bird alive or is it dead?" If the wise man said the bird was alive, then the boy would quickly squeeze the life out of it and present the dead bird to the old man. If the wise man said the bird was dead, then the boy would present the live bird. Either way, they planned to trick the old man and prove him wrong.

The day came when the boys received an audience with the wise man. The one holding the bird asked, "Wise one, is the bird in my hand alive or dead?" The wise man was silent for a moment. Then he bent down until he stood eye-to-eye with the boy and said, "The life you are holding is in your hands."

So it is with the life you hold. And you have the greatest power to control your destiny when you stay single-mindedly focused—"in the zone." Tune out the distractions and tune in to what you love most and what you do best in life. When you place most of your time, attention, and energy into doing the things you love and are the best at, you will eventually reap big rewards. **You hold the key to success in your hands!**

Application

Hopefully you have had quite a journey through this book. You have been introduced to some tools that will be useful in developing your own strategy for success—one step, one goal, and one priority at a time. You'll find that each positive step you take, no matter how small or outwardly insignificant, will stimulate another positive step, until you reach a level of intensity that is unstoppable. All things, even the seemingly impossible, can be accomplished if you:

-✽ Stay focused on what you want.
-✽ Follow your heart's passion.
-✽ Believe in yourself and never give up.
-✽ Prepare for opportunity.
-✽ Ask for what you want.
-✽ Partner with others.
-✽ Connect to the power of a Higher Source.

Affirmation

I am "in the zone" and confidently moving toward my dreams.

Books Available From Robert D. Reed Publishers

Please include payment with orders. Send indicated book/s to:

Name:_____

Address:_____

City:_____ State:_____ Zip:_____

Phone:(_____)_____ E-mail:_____

Titles and Authors	Unit Price
Gotta Minute? The ABC's of Successful Living by Tom Massey, Ph.D., N.D.	$9.95
Gotta Minute? Practical Tips for Abundant Living: The ABC's of Total Health by Tom Massey, Ph.D., N.D.	9.95
Gotta Minute? The ABC's of Effective Leadership by Tom Massey, Ph.D., N.D.	9.95
Gotta Minute? How to Look & Feel Great! by Marcia F. Kamph, M.S., D.C.	11.95
Gotta Minute? Yoga for Health, Relaxation & Well-being by Nirvair Singh Khalsa	9.95
Gotta Minute? Ultimate Guide of One-Minute Workouts for Anyone, Anywhere, Anytime! by Bonnie Nygard, M.Ed. & Bonnie Hopper, M.Ed.	9.95
A Kid's Herb Book For Children Of All Ages by Lesley Tierra, Acupuncturist and Herbalist	19.95
House Calls: How we can all heal the world one visit at a time by Patch Adams, M.D.	11.95
500 Tips For Coping With Chronic Illness by Pamela D. Jacobs, M.A.	11.95

Enclose a copy of this order form with payment for books. Send to the address below. Shipping & handling: $2.50 for first book plus $1.00 for each additional book. California residents add 8.5% sales tax. We offer discounts for large orders.

Please make checks payable to: Robert D. Reed Publishers. Total enclosed: $_____. See our website for more books!

Robert D. Reed Publishers
750 La Playa, Suite 647, San Francisco, CA 94121
Phone: 650-994-6570 • Fax: 650-994-6579
Email: 4bobreed@msn.com • www.rdrpublishers.com